STATE BOARD FOR
TECHNICAL AND
COMPREHENSIVE EDUCATION

NOSTALGIA
SPOTLIGHT
ON THE
FIFTIES

NOSTALGIA SPOTLIGHT ON THE FIFTIES

Michael Anglo

JUPITER BOOKS

First published in 1977 by
JUPITER BOOKS (LONDON) LIMITED
167 Hermitage Road, London N4 1LZ.

Copyright © Jupiter Books (London) Limited and Michael Anglo 1977

SBN 904041 56 5

Composed in Photon Baskerville and
printed and bound in Great Britain by
R. J. Acford Limited, Industrial Estate, Chichester.

Contents

THE
FESTIVAL
OF
BRITAIN

1951

The Festival of Britain

At the time of the festival of britain in 1951 london was still showing a mass of scars from her grievous war wounds. There were vast depressing blitzed sites – charred and derelict buildings, and acres of dusty rubble and brick overgrown with weed – and unsightly decaying air raid shelters disfigured streets and parks. Many public buildings and office blocks, begrimed by soot, fog, and years of neglect, were now pitted and gouged by bomb splinters, and streets of crumbling slum dwellings and patched-up houses were packed with people thanks to the chronic housing shortage. The shops displayed their uninspiring wares limited by austerity and shortages. Goods were in short supply, and a few items, including some foods, were still rationed. All this helped make post-war London a drab and dreary place.

The sanguine belief prevailed that the Festival would give cities and towns hit by the war a face-lift and a boost to their slow recovery. But most of the outward manifestations of the Festival – a few licks of paint here, a few strings of tatty bunting there, and expensive airy-fairy programmes devised by the Arts Council for the benefit of the few – did little to help Britain along, although they did bring a good deal of happiness to display firms, refreshment suppliers, and souvenir manufacturers and sellers, as well as taking the edge off the public's worry about the war dragging on in Korea.

A publisher friend and I spent a boring hour on the South Bank, and the only thing about it that sticks in my memory is a remark he made in the Dome of Discovery when we were told that we could watch the return of radar impulses which were beamed from the top of the Shot Tower and reflected from the moon. He said it would be more useful if it beamed back some cream cheese. I thought at the time that that just about summed up the South Bank.

It had been announced in December 1947 that the Labour Government had decided that the country would celebrate the centenary of the Great Exhibition of 1851 with a festival in the summer of 1951. So a few years after the war nearly £11,500,000 was voted

The festival symbol, as shown on the cover of the official brochure.

toward the project. That is a considerable sum of money even in these days of inflation. It was money which the nation could ill afford.

The Festival of Britain was planned on a nation-wide scale to present the country's contribution to civilization, its traditions and heritage, its creative and commercial potential, and its importance in the post-war world. It all sounded very impressive, but few people outside Britain were impressed.

The main display was built on a twenty-seven-acre blitzed site of a former slum on the South Bank of the Thames between Waterloo and Westminster bridges. Buildings on the site comprised the Dome of Discovery, said to have the largest unsupported roof in the world, 365 feet in diameter, and pavilions devoted to "The Land of Britain", "The Country", "Minerals of the Island", "Power and Production", "Sea and Ships", and "Transport". There were other buildings with exhibits representing "The Seaside", "Health", "Schools", "Sports", "Homes and Gardens", and "British Traditions", the lot just about as boring as old boots for most. There was, of course, the great Festival Hall, the only building to survive the exhibition.

What the significance and purpose, if any, of the lofty bobbin-like Skylon, seemingly balanced on a point, were supposed to be, nobody knew, and though the garish architecture of the buildings and the murals and display designs might have pleased the back-scratching architects and artists who were paid handsomely to produce them, to most of the visitors to the exhibition they just provided a tawdry background for their unexciting ambling around the grounds. There were restaurants, side-shows, and a riverside promenade lined with flags and bunting. From above, the Festival grounds looked like a vast hotchpotch of a circus field, a caravan site, and a building site with work still in progress, divided by an old railway viaduct running right through it. A travel agency advertising in *The Listener* stated that the best idea for the Festival year was a trip to South Africa.

The Natural Scene Pavilion showed the wild-life of Britain and the variety and interdependence of her animals and plants. The Country Pavilion traced how Britons had shaped the landscape until it became "one of the most efficiently farmed countrysides in the world". (That was before motorways and the Common Market.) Shown too was the application of mechanization and science to the breeding of plants and livestock. The Minerals of the Island Pavilion showed the sources of Britain's abundant wealth and the increasing uses to which it was being put. (What went wrong?) The Power and Production Pavilion told the story of the conquest of power, the handling of raw materials, and the structure of British industry. In the Hall of Production were shown the achievements of six main groups of industries – metal-working; woodworking; rubber; plastics, pottery and glass; textiles; and food. Banking, insurance, and commerce got their share of boosting too.

According to the official book of the Festival of Britain, "Britain

builds more ships and a greater variety of them than any other nation.
The contemporary expression of this great tradition is displayed in
the 'Sea and Ships' Pavilion.'' Those were the days. The Transport
Pavilion told the story of road, rail, air, and sea transport, and
telecommunications, when the railways were a service, and one could
dial a number and be connected first time and a telephone did not
cost the earth.

In the Lion and Unicorn Pavilion were illustrated some of the
ideas, beliefs, traditions, and peculiarities which had shaped Britain's
social history and structure, while the Homes and Gardens Pavilion
showed how contemporary designers would serve in the planning
and furnishing of British homes. Out of that came high-rise flats and
plastic cushions. There was also a pavilion devoted to the British

9

The Festival of Britain ship, *Campania*.

contribution to nursing, medicine, surgery, and public health over three hundred years. In the words of a press handout, "Britain has often led the world in the individual attention given to the sick." In those days Britain had a National Health Service that was the envy of most other countries.

Much more entertaining for the public at large were the Pleasure Gardens at Battersea. As the official book said, "London offers enjoyment at Battersea as she formerly did in the Pleasure Gardens of Vauxhall, Cremorne and Ranelagh, where the Londoners of the 18th Century found their amusement and recreation."

At Battersea one could dance, listen to music in the open air, watch ballet, revue, marionettes, or concert parties, and eat and drink indoors or out in all kinds of restaurants. There were flower settings, unusual, fanciful architecture, ornamental lakes and fountains, pavilions, arcades, towers and pagodas, and all sorts of displays. It was Copenhagen's Tivoli Gardens in London.

As well as two theatres for light entertainment – one an open-air amphitheatre seating thirteen hundred, the other a Georgian reproduction by the riverside – a dance pavilion with an extensive floor provided short sessions throughout the day, and there was also music in restaurants. Besides a central garden, a large lawn, and a formal garden surrounded by lavender hedges, there was also a pleasant garden walk alongside the Thames.

In the six-acre amusement park, in addition to the Big Dipper and the Rotor, traditional roundabouts and other rides and all the usual fun of the fair attracted huge crowds. For the very young there was a miniature zoo with a pets' corner, a Punch and Judy show, and a Peter Pan railway.

Among other ingenious attractions was the Tree-Top Walk leading up to a platform with a wide view over the gardens, a fountain tower with its continuous cascade of golden globes instead of water, and a clock tower with working models that operated at the striking of each quarter of an hour. There was also the Grotto in the form of four caves representing Wind, Fire, Earth, and Water, and a complete railway in miniature, five hundred yards long, designed by Rowland Emett, the famous *Punch* cartoonist, with all his characteristic inventiveness and fantasy.

In the numerous shops and kiosks along the Parade and elsewhere, everything from tobacco and toys to perfume and bijouterie was on sale. On a terrace overlooking the river was a luxury restaurant and a wine garden, and in the grounds there were beer-gardens, an English tea garden, and numerous cafeterias and snack bars. In the evenings the gardens were spectacularly illuminated and floodlit, and almost nightly there were firework displays. Battersea Gardens was truly a delight for visitors.

A season of the arts had been planned on a vast scale for May and June in London, a season of music, opera, ballet, drama, and literature. The Royal Festival Hall was to be a permanent example of London's determination to serve not only the world of music, but architecture, painting, sculpture, and literature. The Arts Council had set out to arrange a full representation of the history and practice of British music, the work of orchestras, singers, players, and musical societies from every part of the kingdom and the variety of the nation's musical life, professional and amateur.

The Arts Council commissioned British composers to produce music especially for the Festival, to be included in the repertoire of various orchestras booked for the Royal Festival Hall. In addition to national orchestras there were many from provincial centres such as Bournemouth and Birmingham, Manchester and Liverpool, as well as the Yorkshire Symphony Orchestra and the Scottish National Orchestra.

Leading British conductors, including Barbirolli, Beecham, Boult, and Sargent, appeared in London, as did famous conductors from abroad such as Krips, Koussevitsky, Kubelik, Monteux, de Sabata, and Stokowski. Soloists included Victoria de los Angeles, Claudio Arrau, Clifford Curzon, Suzanne Danco, Kathleen Ferrier, Jascha Heifetz, Pierre Fournier, Myra Hess, Joan Hammond, Leon Goossens, Eileen Joyce, Yehudi Menuhin, William Primrose, Cyril Smith, Solomon, and Jean Tourel.

There were concerts by choirs ranging from small choral groups to massed choirs of more than a thousand voices. Distinguished British and foreign musicians gave song and sonata recitals and chamber music concerts. Serenade concerts were given at Hampton Court, Kensington Palace, Ken Wood, and the Victoria and Albert Museum. There were also programmes of madrigals and of Bach cantatas; organ recitals at Westminster Abbey, St. Paul's, and other churches; brass band concerts; and performances by the English Folk Song and Dance Society and the Pipers' Guild.

The Royal Opera House, Covent Garden, presented the first

A fleet of trucks carried this mobile Festival exhibition round the country.

performance of Vaughan Williams' *The Pilgrim's Progress*, and their Festival season included Wagner's *Der Ring des Niebelungen*, *Parsifal*, and *Die Meistersinger*. Sadler's Wells included two English operas in its programme, Purcell's *Dido and Aeneas* and Vaughan Williams' *Hugh the Drover*, as well as Wolf Ferrari's *The School for Fathers* and three operas by Verdi, *Don Carlos*, *Simone Boccanegra*, and *Falstaff*. The English Opera Group presented the whole of its repertoire of operas by Benjamin Britten – *Albert Herring*, *The Rape of Lucretia*, *Let's Make an Opera*, and the composer's new realization of *Dido and Aeneas*.

There was a Gilbert and Sullivan season at the Savoy Theatre, and at the Mercury Theatre there were productions of intimate opera by Arne, Purcell, Mozart, and Offenbach. At Glyndebourne, four operas by Mozart – *Idomeneo*, *Cosi fan tutte*, *Don Giovanni*, and *The Marriage of Figaro* – were presented.

The Arts Council commissioned a number of new operas in 1951, one by Benjamin Britten, *Billy Budd*, and one by George Lloyd, *John Socman*, performed by the Carl Rosa Opera Company, and others included *A Tale of Two Cities* by Arthur Benjamin, *Wat Tyler* by Alan Bush, *Beatrice Cenci* by Berthold Goldschmidt, and *Deirdre of the Sorrows* by Karl Rankl.

In the programme of the Sadler's Wells Ballet at Covent Garden was *Tiresias*, a work specially commissioned for 1951 with music by Constant Lambert and choreography by Frederick Ashton. The Sadler's Wells Theatre Ballet also performed a new work, *Harlequin in April*, with music by Richard Arnell and choreography by John Cranko. The Festival Ballet Company with Markova and Dolin appeared at the Stoll Theatre in Kingsway, and their programme included *Peer Gynt* and *Atlantic Crossing*, a new ballet to music by Ferde Grofe.

London's drama season was a festival in itself. The Old Vic Company, headed by Peggy Ashcroft, Ursula Jeans, Roger Livesey, and Alec Clunes, presented Sophocles' *Electra*, Shakespeare's *Henry V*, *Twelfth Night*, and *The Merry Wives of Windsor*, Jonson's *Bartholomew Fair*, and Shaw's *Captain Brassbound's Conversion*. At the St. James' Theatre, Sir Laurence Olivier presented a company headed by himself and Vivien Leigh in Shakespeare's *Antony and Cleopatra*, and Shaw's *Caesar and Cleopatra*; John Gielgud played Leontes in *A Winter's Tale* with Diana Wynyard and Flora Robson; Sir Ralph Richardson headed a company in Chekhov's *The Three Sisters*, and Alec Guinness appeared in *Hamlet*. There was a production of James Elroy Flecker's *Hassan*, with music by Delius, and John Clements and Kay Hammond played in Shaw's *Man and Superman*. At the Regent's Park Open Air Theatre there were performances of *A Midsummer Night's Dream*.

Among the new plays presented were *The Golden Door* by J. B. Priestley; *Waters of the Moon* by N. C. Hunter, with Dame Edith Evans and Dame Sybil Thorndike; and *The Thistle and the Rose*, a play about James IV of Scotland by Douglas Home. Three new religious plays were produced in Southwark Cathedral; St. Johns, the Festival Church; and St. Thomas's, Regent Street. This was just part of the programme in the London theatre, which also included music hall, revue, and musical comedy.

The British Film Institute organized the showing throughout the country of the best British films. In London, the New Gallery showed a repertory of British films of the previous fifteen years, with stars, directors, and technicians making personal appearances. In the South

Pulteney Bridge at Bath. The Bath Assembly revived the city's eighteenth-century character for the Festival.

Bank Tele-cinema were shown not only big screen television and the first films ever made combining stereoscopic pictures in colour and stereophonic sound, but also many documentaries especially made for the Festival. Among the feature films released in 1951 were *The Magic Box*, the story of William Friese-Greene, the British film pioneer; *Tales of Hoffmann*; and an adaptation of Joseph Conrad's novel *The Outcast of the Islands*.

The pavilions on the South Bank and exhibitions elsewhere utilized the services of many British painters and sculptors, and the Arts Council commissioned other artists. Sixty were invited to paint large canvases for exhibition in the R.B.A. galleries. There were many special London shows of works by Hogarth, Blake, Henry Moore, and dozens of other famous British painters and sculptors. Galleries all over the country made special features of their art and literary treasures. In Liverpool the Walker Gallery was opened for the first time since 1939 and showed the work of George Stubbs, who was born in the city in 1724, and in the little village of Rottingdean, near Brighton, there was an exhibition of relics of the novelist and poet Rudyard Kipling, who had lived there.

Other cities, towns, and villages had their festivals of music, drama, exhibitions, and sport. At the Shakespeare Memorial Theatre, the season was devoted to a cycle of the Histories – *Richard II*, the two parts of *Henry IV*, and *Henry V* – with the new addition of the *The Tempest*. The company included Michael Redgrave, Richard Burton, Harry Andrews, Hugh Griffith, Rosalind Atkinson, Heather Stannard, and as director Anthony Quayle.

The Bath Assembly, a revival of the city's eighteenth-century character as a centre of taste, fashion, and the creative arts, featured performances by famous British orchestras including the Royal Philharmonic under Sir Thomas Beecham and the Hallé under Sir John Barbirolli. The Bath Choral and Orchestral Society performed *The Dream of Gerontias*, and the Bath Bach Choir joined the London Symphony Orchestra in Handel's *Messiah*. Art exhibitions, literary events, films, and marionette shows for children, were just part of Bath's festival. An unusual feature was the Pageant of Bath performed by local youth groups.

Bournemouth, which had developed through the nineteenth century, solidifying its peculiar charm particularly in the Victorian era, celebrated this aspect of its character in a number of exhibitions accentuating the growth of its taste for art, literature, and architecture. The Winter Gardens featured its own famous Municipal Orchestra and the London Philharmonic. The Sadler's Wells Opera Company and the Sadler's Wells Theatre Ballet appeared at the Pavilion Theatre.

York, Norwich, Worcester, Brighton, Cheltenham, Canterbury, Oxford, and Cambridge all had full Festival programmes emphasizing their rich traditions and taste in the arts. Cardiff, Swansea, Aberdeen, and Edinburgh had music, drama, opera, films, and exhibitions of

Queue for food at reduced prices, 1951.

infinite variety and of the highest quality. Britain was bursting with goodies for lovers of the arts. Edinburgh saw the first visit to Europe in twenty years of New York's Philharmonic-Symphony Orchestra. Its conductors for its fourteen Festival concerts were Bruno Walter and Dimitri Mitropoulos, and among the soloists who appeared with them were Robert Casadesus, Zino Francescatti, Myra Hess, Irmgard Seefried, Rudolf Serkin, and Solomon.

The exhibition theme of the South Bank was considered to be fundamental in expressing the true essence of the Festival of Britain, and in order that its message should reach the main centres of population throughout the country, two travelling versions of the exhibition were created. The ship *Campania* was fitted out with a potted version of the South Bank exhibition, and sundry exhibits on similar lines were packed into a fleet of trucks. The *Campania* visited Southampton, Plymouth, Bristol, Birkenhead, Cardiff, Glasgow, Belfast, Hull, Newcastle, and Dundee. The Travelling Exhibition visited Manchester, Leeds, Birmingham, and Nottingham.

Except for the South Bank exhibition of rubbishy architecture, tatty art, and dull presentations, the Festival in general was certainly stimulating and gave Britain a shot in the arm when she needed it. It started Britain moving out of the post-war doldrums, sometimes into storms but ultimately into the better climate of the late fifties and early sixties. Festival Britain did not dream that in twenty-five years times would be tougher than ever.

15

16

What's showing
at the pictures?

IN 1955 I WAS EDITING AND PRODUCING A MONTHLY FILM MAGAZINE called *Flix*. A number of friends in the film business opened a few doors here and there, and publicity agents and managers were extremely helpful in supplying material. To handle the features I had Eric Linden, an old friend from my *Speedway Gazette* days, who had wisely gone into television, and young Douglas Endersby, who was well versed in public relations and knew his way around the film studios.

It had been a bad time to start a new movie magazine. TV was eating away at cinema attendances, Hollywood after McCarthy was only a shadow of its former self, while the British film industry was in a bad way and always seemed to be undergoing a crisis. The studios at Denham, Highbury, Shepherds Bush, Islington, Isleworth, Bushey, Ealing, Welwyn, Teddington, Hammersmith, and Wembley had closed down, and without Government aid there would have been no British film industry to speak of. British Lion had received financial assistance to the tune of £3,000,000, and even the mighty Rank Organisation was shedding a tear or two and claiming that it was finding it hard to make a crust.

When necessary I visited film sets and went to press shows, but I mostly left that to my wife. Douglas knew Peter Noble well, and what Peter did not know about the film world you could stick under your eyelid and not blink. Gerry Fernback, the jovial and dapper manager of Republic Pictures, helped us in every way he could, and we were never short of film stills and Kodachromes and usually got the pick.

In those days I had met few film actors and actresses other than Roy Rogers, Tex Ritter, and Sabrina, but I soon found that most of the ones I met were extremely helpful. Once I was invited to Nettlefold Studios, where a film was starting production, only to find there was a strike. Paul Carpenter, one of the stars, was playing cards with some stage hands; Bonar Colleano and everyone else was hanging around chatting and smoking and it seemed like a happy party. Later in the restaurant I was introduced to American stars Paul Douglas and Ruth Roman. Paul Douglas seemed a bit fed up, Ruth

Roman was beautiful and charming, but all in all I came away from Nettlefold without much copy and with a vague feeling of depression.

I met Eduardo Ciannelli, the Hollywood actor who always played sinister villains and gangsters, and versatile Sam Wanamaker in Kwei's, the Chinese restaurant in Tottenham Court Road not far from our studios. That and the old Casa Prada in Euston Road were our regular lunchtime haunts. (It was Eduardo Ciannelli who got us hooked on a very superior Wun Tun soup which came at five bob a bucket and was enough to feed a family.) We were often able to pick up a little copy at lunchtime.

Between us Eric, Douglas, and I virtually produced *Flix*, providing colour cover, copy, layouts, artwork, and photographs in what amounted to a day or two as we all had plenty of other things to do. Nobody could turn out copy as fast as Eric, nobody could ferret out stills and grab them before anybody else got a look in like Douglas, and as far as I was concerned layouts and artwork were just so much grist for the mill. My imperturbable assistant, Dorothy Saporito, a brilliant artist, rapidly retouched photos and even knocked out occasional cartoons.

I cannot with honesty say I was particularly enamoured with the job, but it did have its compensations. The first time at Cannes was an experience I enjoyed. It was a novelty, and even in pre-Film Festival days one could drum up some good copy. I picked up an interesting story or two from film actor Maxwell Reed, who was staying at our hotel, and I was on hand when a French film star was brought into the hotel after parachuting into the sea as a publicity stunt. At La Bonne Auberge, the internationally famous restaurant at Antibes, where I went one evening with my wife and young son and a publicity agent with his wife and young son, we met film star Robert Young and his party. Debonair Robert Young is still going strong starring in the TV series "Marcus Welby, M.D.".

A few of the films I remember seeing and enjoying in the service of *Flix* were *The Cockleshell Heroes*; the original *Colditz Story*; *The Dam Busters*; and *Around the World in Eighty Days*, an adaptation of Jules Verne's story in Michael Todd's Todd-AO process on a wide screen. I found *The Cockleshell Heroes* particularly interesting. It was based on a true story about a special commando group of Royal Marine frogmen who were landed by submarine near a French port and then proceeded on a dangerous mission to attach limpet mines to the bottom of German warships.

In the end I left *Flix* for what I thought would be more profitable and interesting ventures, but looking back I must admit that producing a film magazine was one of the easier tasks in which I ever found myself involved.

The fifties were a period of protracted crisis for the film industry.

Kirk Douglas starred as a
New York detective in
Detective Story.

Hollywood's domination was being steadily eroded by serious foreign
competition, with British, French, Italian, and Swedish films creeping
into cinemas all over the world, including the U.S.A., and television was beginning to threaten the power and influence of the
cinema to a degree that shook Hollywood to its foundations. But
Hollywood was not prepared to yield before the fast-growing monster, television, and brought in a host of new weapons to combat
the appeal of its rival.

Many new technical improvements and novelties were tried, some
of which were successful and others not so. There was Cinerama,
CinemaScope, Vista Vision, Todd-AO, stereophonic sound, wide
screens, and some three-dimensional films which had to be viewed
through green and red spectacles. There was even a threat of
"smellies", but this idea was soon dropped as the smells released

19

in cinemas tended to hang about into the following sequences and cause people to eye one another suspiciously. Big-budget spectacular films with huge crowds of extras were produced, which, it was thought, could never be reduced to box size, and, of course, these were in colour, which was still in the embryo stage as far as television was concerned.

The first film to be shown in the CinemaScope process was *The Robe* with Richard Burton, Jean Simmons, Victor Mature, Michael Rennie, and Richard Boone. Based on Lloyd C. Douglas' novel, it was about a Roman tribune ordered to crucify the Messiah and his conversion to Christianity when he donned the robe of Jesus. The production was impressive, but the pace of the film was slow, the dialogue grating and unlikely, and the actors seemed overawed by the grandeur and magnitude of the subject and the knowledge that their images were being blown up to the largest size ever. Hollywood was not alone in feeling the draught through empty cinemas in the fifties. The British film industry was in a chronically unhealthy state. Ealing Studios, which had earned an international reputation for good comedy in post-war years, was forced to close shop and was taken over by the B.B.C. The invariably successful films from Ealing established the screen reputations of a host of comedians such as Alastair Sim, Ian Carmichael, George Cole, Brian Rix, Terry-Thomas, Margaret Rutherford, and Irene Handl. Other British studios closed down, but British film makers stuck to their guns, and directors such as Anthony Asquith and the Boulting brothers continued to make films that were shown throughout the world.

Many of the comedies produced in England had lost all subtlety by the later fifties and had degenerated into the blatant vulgarity of lavatory humour and double entendre, smacking of old-time music hall, which a large section of the British public seem to appreciate. The first of the "Carry On" series, *Carry on Sergeant*, produced at Pinewood by Peter Rogers in 1958, was a huge success and was followed by *Carry on Nurse* in 1959. "Carry On" has become a cult and is still carrying on, on film and TV.

One of the most popular of the comedy stars at the beginning of the fifties was Norman Wisdom, a wistful knock-about comic of the old school whose films for Rank were not memorable.

Genevieve, from Rank, was typical of the better class of film comedy of the fifties. It is about two English veteran car buffs and their wives, entering their cars in the annual Brighton run. The veteran cars gathered together for the film were interesting enough – particularly "Genevieve", a 1904 Darracq, and her rival, a 1904 Spyker – and the antics of the film's leading players, Dinah Sheridan, John Gregson, Kenneth More, and Kay Kendall, and the unusual sequences, were extremely funny. This original film, which has worn well, was an altogether pleasing lighthearted comedy full of wit and charm.

Another typical comedy of this period, *The Captain's Paradise*, with Alec Guinness, Celia Johnson, and Yvonne de Carlo, was adult in its humour, witty and racy. It was about a ferry-boat captain plying between Algiers and Gibraltar, who had two wives, with opposite personalities, one in each port.

A comedy of a different kind was *Hobson's Choice* with Charles Laughton, John Mills, and Brenda de Banzie. Witty and clever, and an excellent vehicle for a masterly performance by Laughton, this film was about the bullying father of three daughters in late-nineteenth-century Salford.

A big success for the Americans was *Marty* (1955). Adapted from Paddy Chayevsky's touching TV drama and directed by Delbert Mann, the film starred Ernest Borgnine and Betsy Blair as two lonely and ordinary-looking people who had almost resigned themselves to being unloved and unwed. The film and Borgnine were awarded Oscars.

By 1955 Hollywood was facing a new and sinister threat to its existence. Senator Joe McCarthy's hysterical anti-Communist campaign was shredding the American people, and Hollywood was coming under heavy fire. There were unbelievable scenes as actors, screenwriters, directors, and leading technicians denounced each other left, right and centre as Communists, crypto-Communists, and fellow-travellers in order to save their own careers or to smash anybody who might be in their way. By self-abasement, self-abnegation and naming friends, acquaintances, and anybody else as left-wing bogey-men, a number of writers accused of having present or past Communist affiliations or of being left-wing sympathizers tried to save themselves from condemnation and ostracism.

Anybody even remotely suspected of Communist leanings, proved or unproved, was blacklisted, which meant that he could no longer work at his job. One of those to suffer was the actor Larry Parks, who had starred in *The Jolson Story*. Anyone refusing to testify when called upon to do so by the House Committee on Un-American Activities could be sent to prison. Screenwriter Dalton Trumbo refused to testify, was sent to prison, and on his release was barred from the studios. However, with the connivance of the more enlightened studio executives, many banned writers continued to write, under assumed names. When the screenplay for *Brave Bulls*, the film with Mel Ferrer and Anthony Quinn, won an Academy Award in 1956, it was an open secret that Trumbo was the mysterious author, "Robert Rich", who could not be located to accept his award, but it was not until Otto Preminger openly commissioned him to write the script for Leon Uris's *Exodus* that Trumbo saw his name in the credits again.

A number of actors, writers, and directors professed pride in their "patriotic" denouncement of "Commies" in the obnoxious McCarthy era, and some of them, self-righteous and smug hypocrites, furthered their careers and feathered their nests by getting rid of talented

Italian glamour girl Gina Lollobrigida, an international leading lady in the fifties.

competitors. After McCarthy castrated Hollywood it was never the same.

An example of film making at its best in the fifties was *The Red Badge of Courage* (1951). It featured two famous personages of World War II as film actors: Audie Murphy, the most decorated American hero of the war, and Bill Mauldin, the American war cartoonist who created G.I. Joe in his series "Up Front" in the service newspaper *Stars and Stripes*. A powerful story about the American Civil War, the film was adapted by Albert Brand from Stephen Crane's novel. John Huston, with masterly skill, transferred the tormenting fears and emotions of a young recruit to the screen. This he did with frightening fidelity within the strait-jacket of attempting to convey in visual terms the book's almost stream-of-consciousness descriptions, a technique that has more realism in a flow of written words than in a series of close-ups of facial contortions to express what is going on in the mind of a young soldier caught up in the ghastly horrors of war.

The main impact of *The Red Badge of Courage* lay in the re-creation of the battlefield near Chancellorville bereft of any false hint of glory, as seen by a pawn in the battle, an ordinary human being thrust into uniform. The ragged, almost decrepit, infantrymen; the noise, smoke, dust, and bedlam of battle; the surging mêlée of cavalry charges and counter-charges; the shattered corpses; the broken men reeling to the rear – all combined to give a whiff of the real stench of war.

The film captured the period look of the Civil War, and each vignette extracted from the screen could have been an old Matthew Brady photograph. The characters, such as the Loud Soldier, the Tall Soldier, and the Tattered Man, their attitudes, the dialogue, and the idioms all seemed vivid and authentic. The film was an indictment of war, and its mark was indelible.

Another film with Civil War overtones made in 1951 was *Red Mountain* with Alan Ladd, Lizbeth Scott, John Ireland, and Arthur Kennedy. A Confederate officer assigned to accompany Quantrell and his Raiders found that Quantrell was not moved by altruism but ruthlessly set on enriching himself with the war as an excuse. Much better was *The Raid*, also about Confederate soldiers but set just after the Civil War. A small band of Confederate prisoners of war who had escaped from a Union prison camp planned the sacking of a small Vermont town as revenge for the destruction of Atlanta in the Civil War. Van Heflin played the implacable Confederate leader, and Richard Boone and Anne Bancroft supported him.

Horror was piling up, with creepy crawlies, buckets of blood, and ghoulies and ghosties from both sides of the Atlantic. Bela Lugosi was still hamming up his share of horrifics and appeared in *The Bride of the Monster*. Dana Andrews and Peggy Cummins, both of whom should have known better, starred in *The Curse of the Demon*, and monsters stomped on in *The Monster That Challenged the World* with Tim Holt, and

Monster from Green Hell, both in 1957. There was even a *Monster on the Campus* (1958). Peter Cushing, Christopher Lee, and Michael Gough were back with Dracula in the *Horror of Dracula* (1958).

But in 1958 the biggest horror was the one staring cinema itself in the face as opinion polls showed cinema attendances falling away to television. All the same, films like *Tiger Bay*, with Horst Buchholz, John Mills, and Hayley Mills, continued to draw full houses. *Tiger Bay* was the film that launched young Hayley on her film career.

The mean streets of old England were providing powerful back-drops for serious British pictures, and *Tiger Bay* showed a good deal of raw Cardiff. Raw themes too showed up well against such back-drops. Tony Richardson's *Look Back in Anger*, with Richard Burton, Claire Bloom, and Mary Ure, adapted from John Osborne's important play, was a powerful commentary on the mood of England in the mid-fifties, highlighting at a crucial time the battle of an angry young man against the establishment. *Room at the Top*, expertly directed by Jack Clayton, depicted the ruthlessness of an opportunist, brilliantly played by Laurence Harvey, determined to get to the top of the heap by fair means or foul, Simone Signoret's superb performance as one of his stepping stones earned her an Oscar. The film had intensity, authentic industrial Yorkshire atmosphere, and a background of corruption that gave it authority and realism.

Hollywood's moguls were still making big box-office attractions, but they were complaining bitterly that they were not making money. Already many skilled film technicians, new writers, and actors were looking to TV for their future, and it began to look as if the old Hollywood masters would not be able to continue for much longer. Fresh blood, new actors, new stories, controversial subjects, and more open sex was needed to boost the film industry, and the Hollywood film maker was no slouch when it came to the crunch.

The Defiant Ones, directed with punch and potency by Stanley Kramer, starred Tony Curtis and Sidney Poitier in a story about two fugitives from a chain-gang, one white and the other black, shackled together and hating the colour of each other's skin. In 1958 that was provocative stuff, and a black star who did not sing, tap dance, touch his forelock, and was not a comic was novelty indeed.

Controversial and abrasive too was *The Young Lions*, adapted from Irwin Shaw's brilliant book about men at war, with Marlon Brando, in one of his best roles, as a pragmatic German, Montgomery Clift as the epitome of persecuted Jewry, and Dean Martin as an urbane, cool, and detached WASP American. Ranging over several countries and theatres of war the film, well made and well acted, brought audiences flocking into the cinema in 1958.

In complete contrast to such solid drama was the sugary confection *Gigi* with Maurice Chevalier, Hermione Gingold, Leslie Caron, and Louis Jourdain. There was music, song, dancing, gaiety, and laughter in this colourful movie, but perhaps there was, too, a faint tinge of decadence. Chevalier played a merry old roué with a rather lecherous liking for little girls, and Caron a girl brought up to be the mistress of a rich playboy, Louis Jourdain. But if the ingredients for the movie were a little unsavoury, they were delightfully cooked.

Blatantly steamy was *Cat on a Hot Tin Roof* with Elizabeth Taylor, Paul Newman, and Burl Ives, adapted and directed by Richard Brooks from one of Tennessee Williams' most powerful studies of the Deep South. Paul Newman as the onetime hero addicted to the bottle, married to Elizabeth Taylor, and dominated by his father, was impressive, and Ives powerfully re-created his stage role of Big Daddy.

A good deal of comedy from Hollywood was of the unsubtle, sledgehammer variety. The slaphappy pair Abbott and Costello were meeting the strangest people. In 1952 came *Abbott and Costello Meet Captain Kydd* and *Abbott and Costello Meet Dr. Jekyll and Mr. Hyde*; in 1955 it was *Abbott and Costello Meet the Keystone Cops* and *Abbott and Costello Meet the Mummy*. In 1956, however, they did not seem to meet anybody but made a film called *Dance With Me, Henry*. Then the team split up and Costello died in 1959.

Abbott and Costello had their large following, but British filmgoers preferred a film such as *The Horse's Mouth*, which in 1959 attracted large audiences in both Britain and America. Alec Guinness and Kay Walsh starred in this chronicle of the misadventures and crazy eccentricities of an artist and his associates. Alec Guinness had previously won world acclaim in *The Man in the White Suit*, thought to be one of the wittiest and most ingenious comedies for years. Peter Sellers was beginning to make audiences sit up and take notice and *The Ladykillers*, in which he appeared with Alec Guinness, established him as a star of vast international potential.

But although stars could still attract audiences they were not always sufficient inducement to bring people flocking to the cinema. Good stories were necessary, and films were made of plays which had scored a success on the stage and whose authors were well known. Terence Rattigan's plays made popular films. His *The Browning Version*, filmed in 1951, was a touching story about a stuffy professor who learnt of his wife's affair with a younger colleague when he was about to take up a post at another school. Michael Redgrave played the professor. Another Rattigan play adapted for the films was *The Deep Blue Sea*. The adaptation, clumsy and laboured, with Vivien Leigh in the role of an emotionally unstable woman attracted to a man beneath her station, played by Kenneth More, did not repeat the success of the stage version.

A crop of good war films, most of them adapted from best-selling books, helped overcome the antipathy to war subjects that had been shown by a large section of the public in the immediate post-war years. By the fifties the reaction to reminders of the war had resolved into nostalgia, curiosity, and a desire to experience the vicarious thrills derived from wartime adventures with their scenes of danger and derring-do.

The Wooden Horse, a British film about the famous escape from

American war hero Audie
Murphy.

Stalag Luft III, was the first of a whole series of escape pictures based on true stories. Leo Genn, David Tomlinson, and Anthony Steel were among the leading players.

Rather more meaty and gruelling was *The Cruel Sea*, adapted from Nicholas Monsarrat's best-selling novel about the men serving on the corvette *Compass Rose*, escorting convoys on the North Atlantic run during the Battle of the Atlantic. It was a penetrating film in many respects. A whiff of class distinction pervaded the wardroom of the *Compass Rose*, which seemed to be very real. Jack Hawkins as Captain Ericson was typically stiff-upper-lipped and upper-bracket; Stanley Baker as Lieutenant James Bennett was definitely an outsider. Worse! He was an Australian who had "conned" himself a commission. What really made him despicable, however, was the fact that he was inordinately fond of the crudest item in the wardroom store cupboard – tinned sausages, known colloquially as "snorkers". Whenever they were served, and that was almost daily, he would exclaim with deep satisfaction, "Snorkers! Good-oh!" (Evidently, unlike his fellow officers, he had never been sent hampers from Fortnum and Mason or Harrods.)

An excellent British drama, *The Desert Rats* (1953), with James Mason and Richard Burton, was loosely based on the famous siege of Tobruk. James Mason was the German "Desert Fox", Rommel, and Richard Burton showed his mettle as the commander of the Australians. Robert Newton played a strange stilted role, that of a soldier who had been a professor in peacetime.

Another desert drama, a few years later, was *Ice Cold in Alex* with John Mills, Sylvia Syms, and Anthony Quayle. The adventures of a tank commander with two nurses on his hands as they made a bid for safety, having to deal with a German spy, to boot, was good entertainment, but was war in the desert ever like that?

Dunkirk (1958), with John Mills and Richard Attenborough, was the story of the epic rescue of the B.E.F. in 1940, told in almost documentary style. The re-creation of the scenes of the evacuation, shot mostly on the south coast of Britain near Rye, had the superficial appearance of authenticity, but the characters were stagey and the dialogue contrived and unreal.

An unusual war film came from America in 1955. *To Hell and Back* was the screen adaptation of Audie Murphy's book about his actual wartime adventures, with some realistic battle sequences and Audie Murphy playing himself and looking the same age as he had been during the war. It was really an amazingly restrained and honest performance by a babyfaced hero, not an actor.

The Bridge on the River Kwai (1957), produced by Sam Spiegel and directed by David Lean, was about the war in South-East Asia. The film told the story of the construction of a railway bridge by British P.O.W.s on the notorious "Death Railway" between Burma and Siam in 1943, and its subsequent destruction by a British Small Operations Group led by Jack Hawkins. Alec Guinness as a humourless British colonel, obsessed with the necessity of proving the discipline and quality of his men, did not even consider that in driving them to work for the Japanese he was guilty of collaborating with the enemy. Jack Hawkins as leader of the S.O.G. was not as patronizingly smug as Ericson in *The Cruel Sea*. William Holden, as one of the S.O.G., did well for the American film market, and Sessue Hayakawa was not too bad a chap for a Jap, in view of the fact that the war had been over for only twelve years. The film was made on location in Ceylon, and the Botanical Gardens at Peradiniya, Mountbatten's H.Q. in World War II, were used for the scenes showing the S.O.G.'s training.

A flashback to World War I was a truly great film brilliantly directed by Stanley Kubrik in 1957, *Paths of Glory* with Kirk Douglas, Ralph Meeker, and Adolphe Menjou. A battered French infantry division at Verdun was ordered to take an almost impregnable German position known as "the pimple", for no better reason than to satisfy the higher command's whim to pretty up their war map. Kirk Douglas gave a fine performance as a compassionate field commander who bitterly resented the inhuman attitude of his superiors and many of his fellow officers and their ruthlessness in dealing with the rank and file. The film was a reminder of how, even in so-called democratic countries, ordinary citizens are conscripted into the army and used callously, even criminally, by governments, the military caste, and their lackeys. What their fate can be for protesting their treatment, often worse than that of animals, was shown in the trial of soldier scapegoats, and their execution by their own comrades, ordered by their class-ridden superiors to cover their own ineptitude, crass stupidity, and bloody-mindedness.

Until his death in 1956 Humphrey Bogart, giant of the forties, was always up front with the biggest stars. *The African Queen* (1952) and *The Caine Mutiny* (1954) were two of his best films, but most of his films were big box-office. In 1950, he made *In a Lonely Place*, a murder mystery, and *Chain Lightning*, in which he played a jet pilot. In 1951 came *Sirocco*, and an excellent Bogart film from 1952 was *Deadline U.S.A.* with Kim Hunter and Ethel Barrymore. It was an absorbing drama about a big newspaper, but without the usual stylized and artificial atmosphere of the city news room. Bogey as an editor had a tough fight on his hands in taking on the Mob and at the same time preventing his publisher, faultlessly played by Ethel Barrymore, from tossing in the sponge. Not too good was *Battle Circus*, (1953), a maudlin war drama, but *The Enforcer*, also from 1953, a semi-documentary about Murder Inc. was more Bogart's style. In 1954 came *Beat the Devil* with Gina Lollobrigida and Jennifer Jones; *The Barefoot Contessa* with Ava Gardner, Rossano Brazzi, and Edmond O'Brien, who won an Oscar for his performance as a loudmouthed press agent; *Sabrina* with Audrey Hepburn, adapted from a hit play; and *The Desperate Hours*, in which Bogart played his last hoodlum role. In 1955, he was in *We're No Angels*, the story of an escape

Katharine Hepburn and
Humphrey Bogart on board
the *African Queen*.

Katharine Hepburn and
Humphrey Bogart on board
the *African Queen*.

from Devil's Island, and in 1956 he starred in *The Harder They
Fall*, a good film based on a novel by Budd Schulberg about the
fight game, with Rod Steiger and Jan Sterling.

In the film version of C. S. Forester's novel *The African Queen*,
directed by John Huston, Bogart starred opposite Katharine Hepburn.
Bogart and Hepburn were never better than in this story of a sticky
journey down crocodile-infested river and leech-infested swamp, by

Clark Gable, Hollywood's "King".

a rough and scruffy waterman and a prim and proper missionary, a lady with a lot of refinement and waspish tongue. In the cramped quarters of the temperamental river craft, plagued by myriad flies and mosquitoes, the unlikely pair started off grating on each other's nerves but wound up recognizing each other's worth and falling in love. The climax of their uncomfortable journey was when they torpedoed a German battleship.

The Caine Mutiny, based on Herman Wouk's novel, featured Jose Ferrer, Van Johnson, Fred McMurray, and Robert Francis. Bogart played the shaky, schizophrenic Captain Queeg of the *Caine* – petty, spiteful, over-meticulous, and without humour, endangering his ship through his own obstinacy and incompetence, and forcing a near mutiny – and in the end was a pitiful figure as he dissolved into incoherence, broken and discredited.

The fifties had a full quota of Western films of every description. By the start of the decade new-look Westerns, featuring hitherto non-Western stars decked out in stetsons, boots, spurs, and gun-belts, superseded the "B" Westerns that were already fighting a losing battle for the young cinemagoer with the new singing cowboys such as Roy Rogers, Gene Autry, and Monte Hale, with their guitars and gimmicky clothes. That is not to say that the new crop of adult Westerns did not have more than enough routine "oaters", as any suffering television critic well knows.

A cowboy star who rode serenely through the forties, the fifties, on through the sixties, and into the seventies, only occasionally deviating from the Western trail, was John Wayne. Already well established, he was on hand in 1950 as a tough cavalry commander in *Rio Grande* with Maureen O'Hara. This John Ford epic was filmed against beautiful scenery, and there were plenty of marauding Indians ready to bite the dust for the delectation of cowboy and Indian buffs of the old school. John Wayne was upriver again in *Red River* (1952), this time as a cattle baron, and yet again, with Dean Martin, in *Rio Bravo* (1959), a dubious mixture of humour and horse manure. Westerns made in the fifties and starring usually non-Western stars included *Across the Wide Missouri* with Clark Gable; *The Naked Spur* with James Stewart and Robert Ryan; *The Last Outpost* with a non-political Ronald Reagan, and Rhonda Fleming; and *Tumbleweed* with Audie Murphy now established as a cowboy in "oaters". Others were *Run for Cover* with cocky Cagney; *Ride Vaquero* with the old heart-throb Robert Taylor and Anthony Quinn; *Seven Angry Men* with Raymond Massey; *Johnny Concho* with a lean Frank Sinatra; *The Tin Star* with Henry Fonda; and *Gunfight at the O.K. Corral* with Kirk Douglas and Burt Lancaster.

Wayne was consistently popular, and only once, in 1958, was he not one of the top box-office draws in the U.S.A. – and that only because he had made few films that year. He is still jogging along, but it is significant that his following has always been a little less discriminating than other movie fans. John Wayne has always been

the screen version of the idealized all-American. Big, tough, mas-
culine, and slow-speaking, he has been especially fitted to play
pioneers of the Old West, American soldiers, and roles where more
brawn than brain was required. The image was preserved with his

xenophobic, rabidly right-wing politics and his denunciation of Communists and anybody else dubbed Communist or left-wing in the McCarthy era, when he openly expressed admiration for the senator.

Typically, Wayne entered the University of Southern California on a football scholarship and graduated to a job in the property department of Fox. He started his film career as an extra on Western film sets, and then came a long haul through bit parts, bigger parts, flops, and a ten-year stint as a Saturday matinée cowboy appearing in dozens of forgettable Westerns. John Wayne even started a career as a cowboy balladeer under the name of Singing Sam, but not surprisingly Sam soon disappeared without trace leaving John to go on making more Westerns and even a few non-Western "B" films. It was in *Stagecoach*, made by John Ford and released in 1939, that Wayne rode into the big time, and he has never looked back since.

A horse opera of a different colour was Delmer Davis' *Broken Arrow*, the first film to show that Indians could be noble heroes, and what was more, such noble heroes that they would be portrayed by painted white men, in this case Jeff Chandler as Cochise, and subsequently by such stars as Burt Lancaster, Rock Hudson, Robert Taylor, and Elvis Presley, to name but a few. With the noble Indian established as a suitable theme for future Westerns, white heroes such as General Custer, the U.S. Cavalry, and pioneers often became villains for cinema exploitation. However, the Redskins were still

Jeff Chandler, Debra Paget, and James Stewart in *Broken Arrow*.

31

made to bite the dust regularly even if they were no longer made to eat dirt.

Commanche (1956) starred Dana Andrews, Linda Cristal, Kent Smith, and bags of Indians. The pesky Indians raided a Mexican town and carried off the beautiful daughter of a Spanish aristocrat, and it was left to Dana Andrews as a cavalry scout to persuade the Indian chief that he came in peace to take back the girl. Dana was given a hard time before he won through. This was the type of Western with traditional whooping movie Indians and the U.S. Cavalry, which was good box-office and had a television future.

Interesting, too, was *The Siege at Red River* (1954) with Van Johnson, Joanne Dru, and Richard Boone, which told the story of the Gatling gun, the clumsy forerunner of the machine-gun, and how it could make the Redskins bite the dust in double-quick time.

John Ford's *Wagonmaster* (1950), considered to be a classic Western with the new look, was a dreary drag by Mormons through frontier territory, relieved only by good scenic photography. As entertainment, the movie was as boring as a long Sunday sermon to seven-year-olds. On the other hand, *The Gunfighter* (1950) was the new-style Western laced with the spicy ingredients of the old ''B'' Westerns for added zest. Gregory Peck played Johnny Ringo, the notorious gunhawk, grown older and wiser, ostensibly sick of killing but more likely realizing that his gun hand and reactions were not what they used to be. Retired from gunslinging, he found himself forced into a shoot-out with a young hoodlum wishing to make a reputation for himself. This theme, well worn in Western movies and accepted as part of the tradition of the Old West, has never been substantiated to any noticeable degree and exists more in legend than in fact.

Every so often somebody delving into the hotchpotch of Western film clichés culled from tired legends and situations and characters of the Old West that never really were, comes out with the true essence of a legend, a piece of old lore, a trace of a hidden story and a sense of authenticity, and blends them with the skill of a folk poet into an inspiring masterpiece of the Western film genre. Stanley Kramer's production of *High Noon*, with Gary Cooper, Thomas Mitchell, Lloyd Bridges, Katy Jurado, and Grace Kelly, was judged by many to be such a film. Carl Foreman wrote the screenplay and Fred Zinnemann directed this Western classic about the courageous and single-minded sheriff of a town made up mostly of worthless citizenry, braggarts and bullies, who was left to face alone a killer and his three cut-throat cronies. The suspense built up with a clock ticking away to the moment of truth at high noon, and in the background the haunting theme, ''Do Not Forsake Me, O My Darling'', sung by Tex Ritter, was evocative of the sombre implications of the taut drama. *High Noon* outclassed the over-rated *Stagecoach*, which has always been much vaunted as a cowboy classic.

Another great Western was *Shane* (1953) with Alan Ladd, Jean Arthur, Van Heflin, Jack Palance, and Brandon De Wilde. The story

Gregory Peck (*right*) as the gunfighter who was never allowed to hang up his guns (in *The Gunfighter*).

33

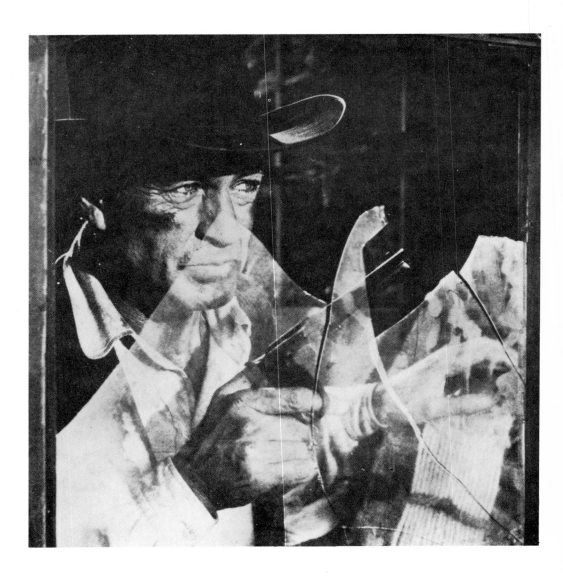

did not amount to much and some of it was pure corn. Set somewhere
in the 1880s, the film was about a gunfighter who came to the
aid of hard-pressed homesteaders. Blank-faced Alan Ladd played
the gunfighter, Shane, skull-faced Palance played a sadistic killer,
but the real interest was in the magnificently photographed scenic
backgrounds.

Best-selling novels have always been a rich source of material
for adapting, compressing, or distorting to make movies. Otto
Preminger's excellent adaptation of Robert Traver's *Anatomy of a
Murder*, starring James Stewart, Lee Remick, Ben Gazzara, and Joseph
Welch, was about a Michigan lawyer who defended an Army officer
accused of killing the man who had attacked his wife. The characteri-
zations were convincing, the dialogue crisp and incisive, and the
overall result a picture of absorbing content.

A less worthy adaptation was the film version of the Broadway
musical based on John O'Hara's *Pal Joey*. Rodgers and Hart provided
the music for this saga of a heel, inimitably sung and played by

34

The amateur, Elisha Cook, Jr., falls victim to the professional, Jack Palance, in *Shane*.

Sinatra. Rita Hayworth just passed muster, Kim Novak was not at her best, and, as is often the case, the film lacked the punch of the original story.

A good cast made up for the soap opera script of *Ten North Frederick*, which was based on another O'Hara book. Gary Cooper, Diane Varsi, Suzy Parker, and Geraldine Fitzgerald were convincing in the roles they had to play, although the sad eyes of Gary Cooper must occasionally have been off-putting to the rest of the cast.

Based on Evan Hunter's best-selling novel about the emerging problem of classroom violence was *The Blackboard Jungle* (1953), with Glenn Ford, Anne Francis, Richard Riley, Vic Morrow, and Sidney Poitier. The film was about a young teacher in a New York vocational school coming up against unexpected violence from his teenage pupils.

More important was *Rebel Without a Cause* (1955), because of the way it influenced impressionable teenagers all over the world and presented them with an identity that suited their egos. For the first time they saw themselves depicted as tough young heroes who were distinguishable from their elders by their argot, clothes, and hair styles. Sullen James Dean was someone they could identify with, emulate, and thereafter blow up into a misunderstood folk-hero. In the film, the young rebels were not the underprivileged sons of slum-dwellers, but the hard-done-by children of well-to-do parents, having everything in the way of material things but professing to lack the real love, understanding, and support of their neurotic parents, who, by the way, had just been through a war. The attitude of these teenagers was blamed on too much privilege. In *The Blackboard Jungle* the kids' behaviour was blamed on their being underprivileged. Whichever way the wind blew, the youngsters liked the attention they were getting from films, the Press, radio, and television, and did their best to live up to the image being created for them. After *Rebel Without a Cause*, they moulded themselves on James Dean, with uniform black leather jackets, jeans, and switchblades. The film set a pattern for sullen, swaggering, would-be-tough teenagers. Now they did not have to play at being cowboys, gangsters, outlaws, or soldiers. They had their own youth hero, not the goody-goody boy hero of the old boys' magazines, but someone who could carry a weapon and showed belligerence not only to authority outside the home, but to his own parents.

Moronic Dean complained in the movie that he was as he was because his father lacked decisiveness and strength, and he whined, "If only he had the guts to knock mum cold once." Judy, his sadistic girlfriend, complained that her tiresome father had stopped kissing her when she was sixteen. Plato, played by Sal Mineo, was drawn to the wild ones because his parents were always leaving him in the charge of the maid. Poor lad. That treatment was enough to try a saint.

Rebel Without a Cause was probably more responsible for producing violence than real violence was for producing the film.

Another film which purported to show contemporary American life was *The Wild One* (1954), based on the story by Frank Rooney. Marlon Brando played the vicious hoodlum leader of one motorcycle gang, and Lee Marvin the gruesomely unstable leader of another, who roared into a small American town and terrorized the inhabitants. Only an ineffectual policeman and a vigilante band were on hand to try to halt the depredations of the grotesquely outfitted hooligans. The film was heavily frowned on in the U.S.A. and was banned from Britain for many years. It was recently shown on television and did not seem to be worth the trouble.

A different aspect of the American scene was shown in *On the Waterfront* (1954), which brought to shivering life the brutal tyranny of the American dockside. Budd Schulberg's screenplay was based on his original story, which was suggested by a series of Pulitzer Prize-winning newspaper articles by crusader Malcolm Johnson. Elia Kazan directed, and Sam Spiegel was the producer.

Marlon Brando, with his slurred speech, was ideal for the role of punchy Terry Malloy and as his brother Charley, Rod Steiger, a newcomer to movies, gave an excellent performance as a money man's lackey. Lee J. Cobb as Johnny Friendly the labour boss typified a worker with power, ruthlessly exploiting his own kind with the help of his goon squads. The longshoremen knuckling under and taking their place in the "shape up", the degrading parade of wage slaves, desperately hoping to be chosen to earn a day's pay; the scenes set

Ava Gardner, voted the world's most beautiful woman in the fifties.

Jaunty detective Naunton
Wayne and Ray Milland in
Circle of Danger.

Jaunty detective Naunton Wayne and Ray Milland in *Circle of Danger*.

in crowded, cold-water walk-up tenements shot on location in
Hoboken; the graft and corruption on the waterfront, near enough
to the truth – were enough to shake the complacency and upset the
consciences of some members of adult audiences, but to most,
seasoned veterans of dozens of gangster, war, horror, murder, and
thriller movies, the film was water off a duck's back. It did not even
put them off their peanuts and popcorn.

Alfred Hitchcock, master of the suspense thriller, was producing
such films as *Stage Fright* (1950); *Circle of Danger* (1951); *Rear Window*
and *Dial M for Murder* (1954); *To Catch a Thief* (1955); *The Man Who
Knew too Much* (1956); and *North by Northwest* (1959).

Stage Fright, a British film with Jane Wyman, Marlene Dietrich,
Richard Todd, Michael Wilding, and Alastair Sim, was an uneven
murder mystery. *Circle of Danger*, another British film, with Ray
Milland, Patricia Roc, and Naunton Wayne, was about an American
returning to Europe to investigate the unexplained death of his brother
in World War II. *Rear Window*, with James Stewart, Grace Kelly,

Raymond Burr, Wendell Corey, and Thelma Ritter, was a suspenseful story spiced with sophisticated comedy and black humour. It concerned a murder witnessed by a temporarily invalided photographer through binoculars from his apartment window.

Dial M for Murder, based on a sensationally successful Broadway play by Frederick Knott, starred Grace Kelly, Ray Milland, Robert Cummings, Anthony Dawson, and John Williams in an exciting mystery drama with a surprising climax. Cary Grant and Grace Kelly starred in *To Catch a Thief*. This story about a jewel thief operating on the French Riviera was not the most exciting Hitchcock comedy

Cary Grant was Grace Kelly's co-star in another Hitchcock production, *To Catch a Thief*.

Popular singer and comedienne Doris Day played a more dramatic role in the thriller *The Man Who Knew Too Much*.

thriller, but with its spectacular Riviera backdrops and tangy atmosphere it was adequate entertainment.

The Man Who Knew too Much, with James Stewart and Doris Day, was suspenseful and action-packed from the beginning to the end with intrigue, murder, assassination plots, and kidnaps. This was Hitchcock ranging near his best, but in *North by Northwest* he scored a bull's-eye. Like the brilliant artist he could be he splashed his vivid scenes back and forth on a broad canvas stretching from the

Oak Room in the New York Plaza Hotel to Mount Rushmore with its gigantic heads of the American presidents carved by Gutzon Borglum in the solid rock. Made with tongue in cheek, the film was about a Madison Avenue advertising executive, played by Cary Grant, who was mistaken for a Federal Intelligence agent by foreign spies and found himself chased from pillar to post by the sinister villains of the other side, as he was being used by the F.B.I. for their own nefarious purposes. Not unnaturally upset by the whole caper, he decided to defend himself against all comers, including Eva Marie Saint, his romantic vis-à-vis. James Mason played the urbane leader of the enemy spy team, and Leo G. Carroll, as Chief of American Intelligence, showed his suitability for future promotion to chief of U.N.C.L.E.

More conventional was *Detective Story* (1951) with Kirk Douglas and William Bendix, adapted from Sidney Kingsley's Broadway play and directed by William Wyler. Kirk Douglas was convincing in his portrayal of a sullen, cold, dedicated detective in a New York precinct, brutalized by his dealings with criminals over the years. This was not the slick, smart-aleck private eye of never-never land, nor the standard detective of the typical movie precinct station, but a believable person.

Far less likely was *Touch of Evil* (1958), another kind of detective

The massive Orson Welles kills Akim Tamiroff over the bed of a drugged Janet Leigh in *Touch of Evil*.

41

Cyd Charisse, long-legged
American dancer born Tula
Finklea.

The talented Gene Kelly, dancer and choreographer supreme.

story, redolent of tequila and garlic and set in the seedy backstreets of Tijuana. Orson Welles wrote and directed the movie as well as playing a leading role as the gross, repellent, and crooked detective investigating a murder. Other contributors in this bizarre story of vice and sleaziness were Marlene Dietrich, Joseph Cotton, Akim Tamiroff, and Mercedes McCambridge.

Two of the best musicals of the fifties starred the versatile and engaging Gene Kelly, dancer, choreographer, and singer, and an outstanding figure in the post-war musical scene. These were *An American in Paris* and the immortal *Singing in the Rain*, which were full of unforgettable "buzz around the brain" tunes and slick dance routines.

An American in Paris, directed by Vincente Minnelli, featured the young Leslie Caron in ballets performed on the lavish sets of a garish but plausible Hollywood Paris. Gene Kelly was a young expatriate American artist bursting with exuberance and singing, whistling, humming, and dancing happily on his bouncy way. Oscar Levant as his long-suffering friend was humorous in a melancholy way, and Nina Foch played the sophisticated, svelte American lady willing to buy the young artist's pictures as the price of his love. George Gershwin's music, with such numbers as "Our Love Is Here to Stay" and "I Got Rhythm", and the brilliant score that included his "American in Paris" suite for the final flourish of the big ballet scene, wrapped the whole delightful package in a gift-wrapping of melody.

Metro-Goldwyn-Mayer's *Singing in the Rain* (1952), with Gene Kelly directing, dancing, and singing gleefully to music provided by Harold Rossor, Nacio Herb Brown, and Roger Edens, is probably one of the best musicals ever made. A satire on the transition in the late twenties from silent movies to talkies in Hollywood, the film raised more than a few laughs, with mobile Donald O'Connor providing a big quota. There was the famous sequence in which Kelly slopped like a happy kid through the puddles in belting rain, dancing and singing the title song, the recorded sound-track of which sold in hundreds of thousands; Donald O'Connor's slick acrobatic dancing in "Make 'em Laugh"; Kelly and O'Connor clowning "Moses Supposes"; lavish production numbers including the spectacular grand finale "Broadway Ballet" danced by Kelly and Cyd Charisse, the girl with the gorgeous legs. Cute Debbie Reynolds more than held her own, dancing along with all of them, and Jean Hagen was perfect as the dumb-blonde star of silent films whose high-pitched, nerve-racking voice presented her with a problem of which she was blissfully unaware.

Another film that pleased lovers of musicals was *The Band Wagon*, directed by Vincente Minnelli, with Fred Astaire, Cyd Charisse, Jack Buchanan, Oscar Levant, and Nanette Fabray. Fred Astaire played a fading Hollywood star ready to make a comeback in a Broadway show produced by temperamental Jack Buchanan. Fred and Cyd performed "Dancing in the Dark" in Central Park; Fred and a Negro shoeshine boy danced a slick number, "Shine on my Shoes", in a New York amusement arcade; and Fred and Cyd, probably Astaire's best ever dancing partner, got together for that usual ballet finale, this one called "Girl Hunt Ballet". Most of the tunes in the movie were familiar Howard Dietz and Arthur Schwarz numbers.

Haunting music highlighted Charles Chaplin's film *Limelight* (1952). A legend in his own lifetime, Chaplin was seen as a philosopher and a pundit by many people, who found in any new Chaplin film some complex social issue; some profound philosophy in the obvious, such as a simply expressed conflict between the "little man" and the all-powerful juggernaut of mechanized civilization; some hidden truths in maudlin manifestations of human frailties and paradoxes. However, *Limelight* was a simple, quiet, mellow, amusing, and altogether pleasant film with very little new to say. An outstanding comedy scene was a burlesque pantomime with Chaplin as a violinist accompanied by Buster Keaton on the piano. Young Claire Bloom played the heroine. Chaplin's usual pathos, poignancy of scene, and comedy business found plenty of expression in this story of an old trouper on the skids.

Audrey Hepburn, Belgian-
born star of Irish-Dutch
parentage who rose to
Hollywood stardom as an
elegant gamine.

45

One of the big guns used by the film companies in their battle with television was the spectacular with thousands of extras and far-ranging settings. Paramount's *War and Peace* (1956) was a game attempt to bring Tolstoy's masterpiece to the big screen, complete with the Battle of Borodino, the burning of Moscow, and Napoleon's long retreat. Audrey Hepburn was perfect as Natasha, Herbert Lom adequate as Napoleon, and Mel Ferrer passable as Prince Andrei; but Henry Fonda, although plausible enough, was perhaps a little too lean for Pierre Bezuhov. Like most epics made in the fifties, the film concentrated on spectacle rather than characterization and depth.

Other epics, such as Cecil B. De Mille's *The Ten Commandments* (1956) and Sam Zimbalist's *Ben Hur* (1959), were box-office boosts, but spectacle alone could not make up for poor acting and dialogue, and a biblical tale with strong American accents can be very off-putting.

The Ten Commandments told the story of Moses from the time he was discovered in the bullrushes until he climbed Mount Sinai to receive the Commandments. The cast, almost as impressive as the subject, but perhaps overwhelmed by the portentousness of the biblical content, did not display any of their undoubted acting ability: perhaps they were inhibited by the words put in their mouths by irreverent scriptwriters. Charlton Heston, Yul Brynner, Ann Baxter, Edward G. Robinson, Yvonne de Carlo, Debra Paget, John Derek, Sir Cedric Hardwicke, Nina Foch, Vincent Price, and John Carradine all managed to slip thin slices of ham into this giant Jewish meal. The result was that it did not seem Kosher.

Based on Major-General Lew Wallace's novel, *Ben Hur* was a remake of the 1925 film which had starred Ramon Navarro and Francis X. Bushman. Charlton Heston played the Jewish prince converted to Christianity, the role previously played by Navarro, and Stephen Boyd was Messala, his Roman rival, in place of Francis X. Bushman. Everything was more or less faithfully replayed, including the famous chariot race. The dialogue was a little more literate than that in *The Ten Commandments*, but the intensity and youthful good looks of Navarro and the gleaming eye of Francis X. Bushman in the first version of *Ben Hur* could not be matched in the second.

A different sort of spectacular was another remake, this time of an earlier version of De Mille's *The Buccaneer*. Again Charlton Heston headed the cast, with Yul Brynner, Inger Stevens, Charles Boyer, and Claire Bloom, and once again Jean Lafitte the pirate (Brynner) came to the aid of Andrew Jackson (Heston), but with a little less swash-buckling than in the original movie. However, the lavishness of the De Mille production, which was directed by Anthony Quinn, and the strong cast, compensated in part for lack of pace and credibility.

Pin-up girl and sex symbol of the fifties *par excellence* was the ill-starred Marilyn Monroe. The picture showing her with her skirt blown

above her waist became famous all over the world. She appeared in the comedies *We're Not Married* and *Monkey Business* (1952) and *How to Marry a Millionaire* (1953), but is probably best remembered for her roles in Billy Wilder's *Some Like it Hot* (1959), with Tony Curtis and Jack Lemmon, and *The Seven Year Itch* (1955), with Tom Ewell, thought by many to have been her best screen performance. She also starred in *The Prince and the Showgirl* opposite Laurence Olivier in 1957.

A more typical Olivier performance was in *Richard III* (1959), with Claire Bloom, John Gielgud, and Ralph Richardson. Shakespeare's powerful study of the physically and mentally stunted king and his machiavellian machinations was brilliantly acted, particularly by Olivier as the epitome of evil.

Cyrano de Bergerac, made by Stanley Kramer in 1950, directed by Michael Gordon with a screenplay written by Carl Foreman, was the only film of the swashbuckling genre in which the star could also act. For his role as the flamboyant, long-nosed, big-mouthed Gascon, Cyrano, Jose Ferrer deservedly won an Academy Award

47

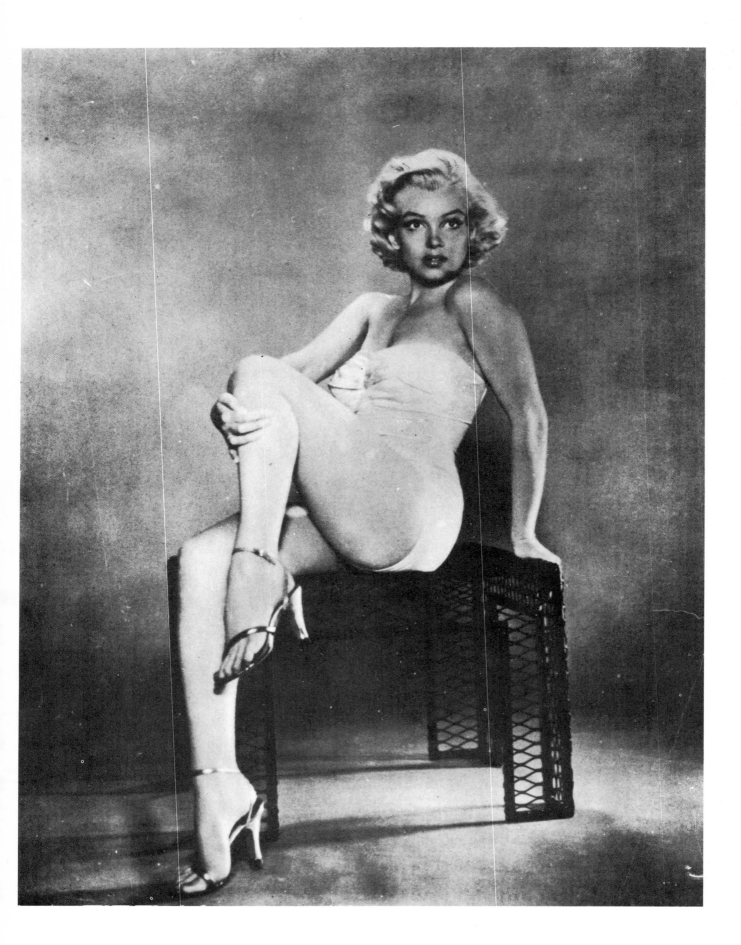

48

as the best actor of the year. The film was broadly based on Edmond
Rostand's fictional verse comedy written in 1897, in which Ferrer
had starred on Broadway in 1946. An interesting fact about this film
was that Ferrer and other members of the cast were coached in sword-
play for the duelling sequences by Fred Cavas, who in his time
had instructed the greatest of all swashbucklers, Douglas Fairbanks
and Errol Flynn. The story was about a soldier of fortune with
an outsize nasal organ, obviously a phallic symbol, and his unre-
quited love for the lovely Roxanne. Cyrano de Bergerac actually
lived from 1619 to 1655. A soldier until the age of twenty, he became
an author, and his propensity for duelling and other escapades gave
him a reputation as a romantic hero.

Typical of the Italian neo-realistic school of filming was *La Strada*
(1956), which showed the talents of Federico Fellini as a director
as well as a story and screenplay writer. American actors played
leading roles in this Italian film produced by Dino de Laurentiis

49

Wonderful Things, filmed on location in Gibraltar in 1958, starred Jeremy Spenser, Jackie Lane, and Frankie Vaughan.

and Carlo Ponti which was about a brutish itinerant third-rate strong-man performer who took on a dull-witted waif as his stooge, cook, and bed-mate and dragged her around the Italian countryside in his decrepit motorcycle trailer to seedy fairgrounds. Anthony Quinn as the scruffy strong-man, and Richard Basehart unlikely as a clown, were the Americans, and Giulietta Masina played the girl.

By the end of the fifties, smaller cinemas specializing in foreign films such as this were becoming all the vogue.

A bookman's bonanza

IT WAS IN THE FIFTIES THAT I STARTED ACCUMULATING AN extensive library of mainly contemporary books. For the first time in my life I was able to purchase hardbacks as they were published, more often than not acquiring them a few weeks prior to publication from a friend in the book business. I had never been able to keep paperbacks, regarding them as expendable and handy to fob off on inveterate book borrowers, and I relied heavily on libraries for serious reading matter and research material. About 80 per cent of my books are non-fiction and include biographies, classics, a number of technical manuals, a collection of cookery books from all over the world, and reference books. The rest are novels, mostly by contemporary American authors.

In the fifties many books about World War I and World War II were published, fiction and non-fiction, books such as *From Here to Eternity; The Naked and the Dead; The Young Lions;* and *Battle Cry; Defeat into Victory; The Memoirs of Field-Marshal the Viscount Montgomery of Alamein; The Turn of the Tide; In Flanders Fields;* and *1914.* I bought many books on the wars, but rarely books about naval warfare or the experiences of P.O.W.s.

I read with fleeting interest books such as Thor Heyerdahl's *Kon-Tiki,* reminiscent of the adventure books of my schooldays. Heyerdahl, a Norwegian ethnologist, had put his theory of the flow of races to the test by drifting across the Pacific with six companions on a raft of balsa logs. The expedition, well publicized, captured the public imagination and the book was a best seller. I browsed through other escapist books, such as Maurice Herzog's *Annapurna* and *The Silent World of Jacques Cousteau,* without much enthusiasm, although I find Cousteau on television absorbing. I preferred books like James Cameron's *1914,* in which the subject matter was far ranging and the author an experienced far ranger.

James Cameron was the chief foreign correspondent and international affairs columnist on the *News Chronicle* in the days when it was a real newspaper. In his book he re-created the Britain of 1914, bringing into clear focus the year which started with the country superficially prosperous, confident, proud, cocky, and at peace, and ended with it shocked by the enormity of the terrible task it had undertaken and the morass in which it found itself, with the spectre of defeat, something never dreamed of, hovering in the background.

Cameron knew war at first hand and had travelled widely. He had been attached to British forces in all theatres of war, and had been with the American Navy in the Pacific, the American Marines in Korea, the French Foreign Legion in Indo-China, the Chinese in China, and the Russians in Russia. He was reputed to have an impartial distaste for all of them, which made him a man after my own heart.

I admire John Masters, author of *Bhowani Junction* and *Nightrunners of Bengal*, and a particular favourite of mine is his *Bugles and a Tiger* (1956), a vivid account of Masters' own experiences as a young officer in a Gurkha regiment between 1934 and 1939. This autobiography, pithy, blunt, and at all times gripping, was chock full of interesting accounts and descriptions of Gurkha regimental life and customs, not without humour, and of grim warfare on the North West Frontier. The book had the feel of India – the essence, the sounds, the smells, the cold, the heat, the monsoons, and the indefinable atmosphere of the Indian sub-continent.

I liked Rayne Kruger's *Goodbye Dolly Gray* (1959), the story of the Boer War. The well-known song that gave the book its title still evokes the last years of the Victorian era, and the war in South Africa with its legendary events and figures such as the Relief of Mafeking, Spion Kop, Kruger, Kitchener, Rhodes, and Baden-Powell.

Books, both fiction and non-fiction, which delved into the inner workings of big business had their peculiar fascination. American writers seem to have the knack of illustrating the machiavellian processes of the harsh world of business, turning the spotlight on everything from films to groceries either in exposés or through fiction.

Vance Packard's *The Hidden Persuaders* was an exposé of the use in advertising of techniques of mass persuasion through the unconscious. A graduate of Columbia School of Journalism, Packard became interested in the work being done by the Institute for National Research in New York State, and collected material on the subject of motivational research from all over America. His book exposed the sinister processes evolved and applied in the field by American super-advertising men. It was written in 1956, and the idea that "brain washing" processes have diminished in the twenty years since is only a fallacy.

Turning to fiction, *The Wall to Wall Trap* by Morton Freedgood was a sardonic, savage story of a successful American film publicity executive trapped in the rat race, habitually cringing, anticipating a knife in the back, in the lush world where Martinis and blondes were on the expense account. And *Expense Account* was the title of Joe Morgan's book about the schizophrenic life of a young American sales executive who lived the life of Riley on his business expense account, eating caviare and drinking champagne at the best restaurants and staying at the best hotels, but having to return every so often to the reality of his small suburban home where his wife struggled to pay the bills out of his inadequate income.

A hard look at the American shoe industry was *The Spiked Heel* by Richard Marsten, a novel about Kahn's Fashion House, a family business manufacturing fashion shoes which was taken over by a huge shoe combine. Marsten used a sharp cobbler's knife to strip away the smart uppers and expose the shabby inner soles of the shoe industry, where a power-crazy Jeff McQuade can move in and ruthlessly eliminate opposition, placing "yes men" in key positions.

Harvey Howells, who came from Scotland and became an American citizen in 1946, was an advertising manager until he gave up big-city advertising to be a writer. He wrote plays for television, one of which won the 1956 Writers' Guild Award for the best television comedy of the year. His novel *The Big Company Look* was about a large grocery business, and as in Marsten's book, the theme was brutal ruthlessness and intrigue in the struggle for power. Jackson Pollet was the boy wonder of merchandising who changed from a personable young man to a tyrant in his climb to the top, sacrificing friends, marriage, and integrity along the way.

The Admen, a novel about the American advertising business, was written by Shepherd Mead, who knew his subject from bottom to top. Until retiring at the age of forty-one to take up full-time writing, he was for five years one of the thirty-eight vice-presidents in an enormous New York advertising agency. *The Admen*, his first novel, sold nearly three million copies in hard covers. Mead was also the author of the tongue-in-cheek guide *How to Succeed in Business Without Really Trying,* an international best seller. Having worked for a while in an advertising agency as a visualizer, ideas man, and copywriter, I found Mead's books particularly interesting.

While I was at the agency I became interested in cookery, and throughout the fifties I collected cookery books and menus from all over the world and acquired a number of sections of André Simon's *Guide to Good Food and Wine*. When it was published in one volume in 1956, completely revised, I bought a copy. It is a concise encyclopedia of gastronomy, and for a number of years it was my gastronomic vade-mecum.

Mediterranean and French Country Food by Elizabeth David, first published in 1950, describes regional cooking in France and is a pleasure to read even for those with no knowledge of cooking. *The Complete Italian Cookbook (La Cucina)* by Rose La Sorce is one of my favourites, although it is completely without illustrations. But the recipes, easy to follow, really do work. *Jewish Cookery* by Leah W. Leonard, first published in 1951, was another cookbook that made mouth-watering browsing and contained just about everything from soup to nuts. It was also in 1951 that I purchased my first Fannie Farmer *Boston Cooking School Cookbook,* first published in 1896. This fat book was bursting its binding with juicy recipes, and one could go through life cooking happily from this cookery book without

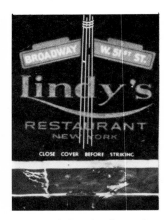

A souvenir book of matches from Lindy's, the restaurant made famous by Damon Runyan.

recourse to any other. I still find it a good book for bedtime browsing.

The Art of Jewish Cooking by Jenny Grossinger, first published in America in 1958, was very amusing. Jenny Grossinger, famous for putting the Catskill Mountains on the resort map with Grossinger's, was each year pulling in fifty thousand guests hankering after good cooking and plenty of it. This cookbook had recipes for anything from Chicken Chow Mein and Chinese Sweet and Sour Meatballs to Chile Con Carne and Pizza. Well, how Jewish can you get?

James Beard's Fish Cookery (1955) was a comprehensive, authoritative work by a well-travelled author who knew the art of buying and preparing fish, and covered the ways of cooking fish from court bouillon, chowder, and bouillabaisse to chiberta. These were the days before plastic fish fingers, and browsing through Beard's book one is engulfed in waves of nostalgia for fish and chips the way they used to be when fish shops were frying six nights a week.

In the fifties I was able to buy reprints of books I had not been able to afford before. Among them were *Ulysses* and *Finnegan's Wake* by James Joyce, *The Wings of the Dove* by Henry James, and the omnibus editions of Damon Runyon, my favourite author. These were *Runyon on Broadway* and *Runyon from First to Last*, which included collections I already had and knew practically by heart. In New York I went several times to Lindy's, the restaurant on Broadway which Runyon had made famous in his stories as Mindy's, and while eating gefüllte fish it seemed as though I was able to recapture in part the atmosphere of the Runyon days. Lindy's has since gone, but I can still find Mindy's in Runyon's books, and meet Harry the Horse, Big Nig, Spanish John, Little Isadore, and Nathan Detroit.

The British were publishing more books than any other English-speaking people in the fifties, and many of the authors published in Britain were American. The fastest-growing fields were educational and non-fiction books. Television was beginning to make people read less, but television and films were rich mines for well-publicized and successful authors. Authors with an eye on film and television rights angled their stories for adaptation for the large and small screens, and many of the public did not seem to mind reading a book, seeing it as a film, and seeing it again as a television serial, or conversely seeing a film and reading a book based on a TV series.

Peyton Place by Grace Metalious was a large novel about a small community, with small-minded people, in a small New England town full of strange characters with stranger hang-ups, skeletons in the cupboards, nasty habits, and hasty hates, as well as a few do-gooders and respectable folk. Everything happened in Peyton Place, and the chronicle of scandal of every description was a natural for television.

One of the most successful American novels of the decade was *The Catcher in the Rye* by J. D. Salinger, a Jewish New Yorker who for reasons of his own disdained all offers to have his book turned into a movie. It was about a wistful adolescent boy roving around New York describing in a matter-of-fact way a series of strange adventures involving taxi-drivers, nuns, an elevator jockey, some girl visitors from Seattle, a prostitute, and an ex-teacher.

John O'Hara, author of *Appointment in Samarra* and *Pal Joey*, wrote *Rage to Live*, *Ten North Frederick*, and *From the Terrace*, all best sellers, in the fifties. *Ten North Frederick* was a family history about Joe Chapin and his wife, but O'Hara, with the skilled dexterity of a surgeon, wielded his pen like a scalpel to bare the innermost secrets of the citizens in Joe's town, then with the uncompromising detachment of a camera cruelly recorded the revelations – their motivations, loves, casual sexual diversions, and aberrations. Here again, with its dirty politics, titillating infidelities, and sexual overtones and undertones, it was rich fruity pudding to serve up as a movie, and with Gary Cooper to play the doleful Joe Chapin, how could it miss? But somehow it did.

More ambitious was *From the Terrace*, a substantial story of big business, politics, and the infra-structure of millionaire society. It was the life story of what is still regarded as the archetypal hero of modern times. Alfred Eaton, successful in politics, business, and love, a millionaire, found that millionaires too have their social strata and in the end realized that to a multi-multi-millionaire he was just a stooge.

James Gould Cozzens was born in Chicago in 1903 and went to Harvard, where in his first year he completed a novel, *Confusion*. Painstaking and competent, he continued to write novels except for a three-year stint writing manuals and speeches for the Army Air Corps in World War II. Cozzens, who showed a deep understanding of people in all his works, scored a big success with *Guard of Honor*, an earthy novel about three tense days at an air base in Florida in 1943, which won him a Pulitzer Prize in 1948. His controversial, intellectually stimulating *By Love Possessed* (1959), adjudged to be one of the finest novels of the century, took seven years to write. It was the story of two days and one hour in the life of Arthur Winner, taking the reader deep into the recesses of the mind of a remarkable man. For two days the world was the familiar one Winner had always known, solid, plainly etched, and absorbing, but the revelations of the one additional hour brought Winner face to face with the deeper meanings of the world and himself. The sudden impact of a four-letter word in its context in the penultimate chapter was shattering in its effect.

It took almost a decade after World War II for many men who had something to say about it all to gather their thoughts and settle down to write, seriously, usually in the form of fiction solidly based on experience, about what they had seen and thought during the war: sometimes angry and bitter, sometimes disillusioned and cynical, and sometimes critical, self-righteous, and wise with hindsight, but often with deep penetration, compassion, and humour, and at times with more sorrow than anger. Articulate soldier-writers put into words their war, how they saw it, to show those who had not seen it how it was.

James Jones had joined the American Army in 1934 soon after leaving school. He was serving at Schofield Barracks not far from Pearl Harbor when the Japanese struck from the air on December 7, 1941. He was made up to corporal in 1942 but was busted eighteen months later. In 1944 he became a sergeant, but was busted again. He was wounded at Guadalcanal. It took him eight years to write his first novel, *From Here to Eternity*, which raised a good deal of controversy in the United States because it was highly critical of the U.S. Army and showed it, like every other army, to be riddled with hide-bound traditions, incompetent and bone-headed officers, stupid regular soldiers, and prejudice. The novel dealt with the few days preceding the bombing of Pearl Harbor and concentrated mainly on the lives of five people in and around Schofield Barracks. Jones' style, eminently readable, vivid, realistic, and arresting, sometimes lapsed into unlikely dialogue as when Warden, a regular soldier and not exactly an intellectual, just out of bed with Karen, wife of his superior officer, was shown a scar on her belly and treated to a lengthy discourse on the meaning of "hysterectomy". Poor Warden. He must have wondered whether the quick jump into bed was worth the lecture.

Jones' next book, *The Pistol*, a short work published in 1958, seemed to have been written as a stop-gap between *From Here to Eternity* and his next novel, *Some Came Running*, which took six years to write. The latter was a massive work about a middle-aged ex-soldier turned writer returning to his hometown after an absence of nineteen years to find he is a misfit in the world where his brother smokes only fat expensive Uppman Havana cigars. In the film based on the book, Frank Sinatra was the unlikely choice to play the stout, balding, middle-aged writer.

Norman Mailer's *The Naked and the Dead* (1949) was said by George Orwell just before he died to be "the only war novel of any distinction to appear hitherto". This was an extravagant assessment. Mailer's moral crusading and altruism prompted by a passionate and almost fanatical resolve was evident when he wrote of war, and the realism of his descriptions cannot be denied, but the realism of his soldiers' dialogue was often off key as when, in those hypocritical days when certain words could hold up publication of a book, euphemisms had to be used in the case of the ultimate in four-letter words, making a frigging nonsense of soldier talk.

Human fallibility was Mailer's subject in *The Deer Park* (1957), which concerned the characters, habits, and morals of the Hollywood movie élite taking their pleasure and relaxation in a Californian desert resort. It was a long cry from the realism of the battlefield in *The Naked and the Dead*, but Mailer's study of people in more

rank Sinatra starred in
me Came Running in 1958.

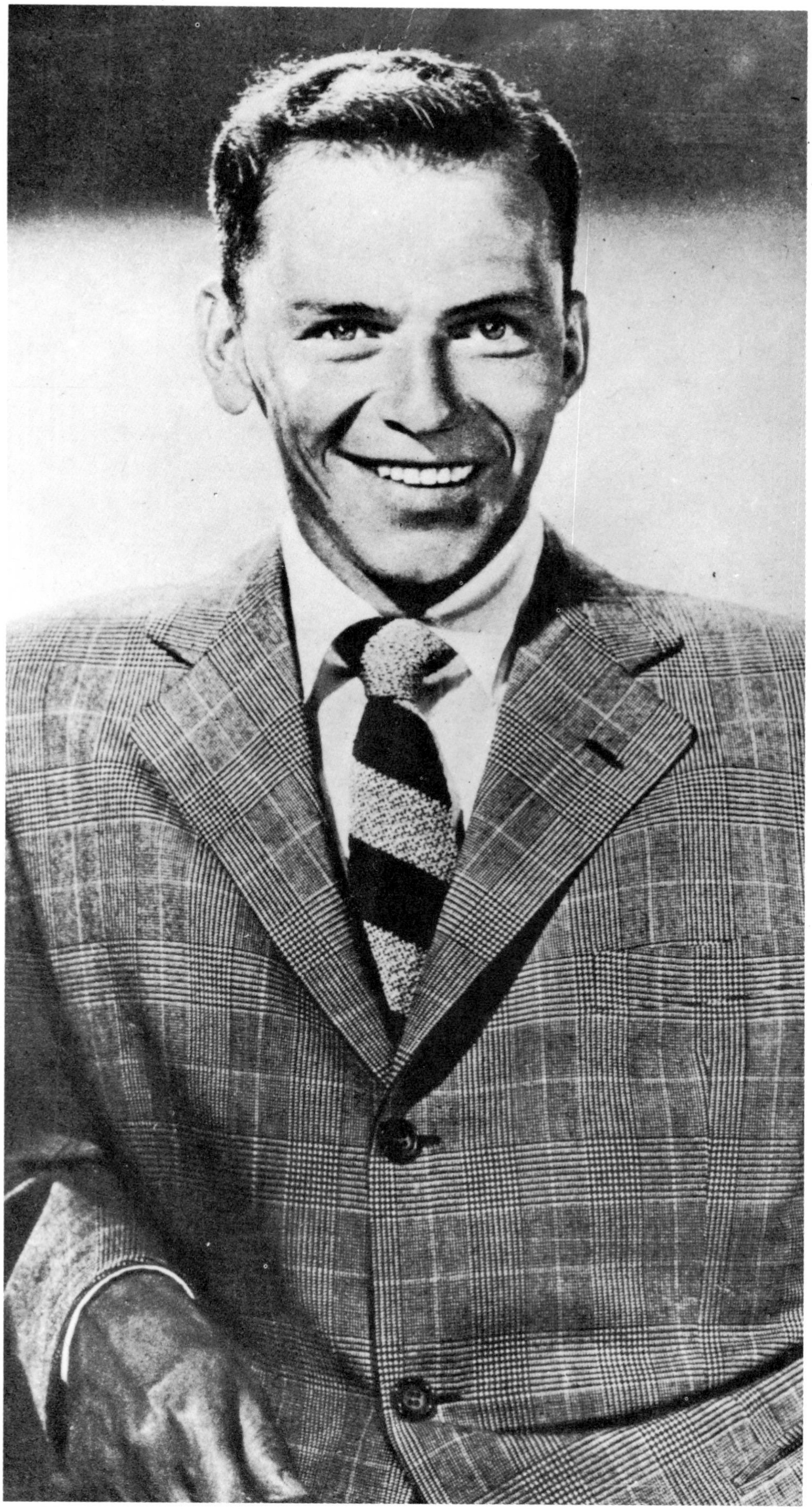

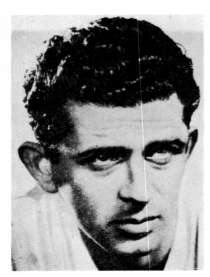
Controversial novelist
Norman Mailer.

lush circumstances was just as analytical and ruthless, and his moral judgements just as sure.

The Young Lions by Irwin Shaw had, in 1949, been greeted with enthusiasm by the critics. It was an engrossing novel on a grand scale about the campaigns in North Africa and Europe seen through German as well as American eyes. Shaw's soldiers were mostly human beings, rarely subhumans, and despite the atrocities and obscenities of the war which Shaw recounted faithfully, somehow through his characters, with their conflicts of national and personal loyalties, he managed to achieve a measure of philosophical synthesis – very difficult to do just a few years after the bitterness of the war and the subsequent exposure of German bestiality and depravity.

Shaw, like Mailer, left the war far behind in his next novel, *Lucy Crown*, which was about a human triangle: not husband, wife, and lover, but the one more familiar in real life and less usual as a subject of fiction, that of mother, husband, and offspring.

Another best-selling American book about World War II was *Battle Cry* (1953) by Leon Uris, who had served in the war as a U.S. marine. Here again were fictionalized true experiences by an ex-serviceman, but less familiar to readers of war literature were the experiences of U.S. Marines in Australia and New Zealand prior to the assault on the Japanese South Sea islands, when tension between U.S. servicemen and Anzac troops returning from the Middle East often resulted in brawling and bloody fights between them.

Exodus (1959), another American best seller, and deemed by many to be an infinitely better book than *Battle Cry*, established Uris as one of the major writers of the decade. Graphic and detailed, yet sometimes seeming a little off key, the book was practically a history of the foundation of the State of Israel. Writing with passion and patriotic verve for the new state, almost fanatical at times, Uris unequivocally denounced the British Government and its Palestine administration, whose unsavoury activities in the formative days of the state were motivated solely by expediency. Many British readers were angry and ashamed that so many of their own political and military leaders should have acted so inhumanely after the holocaust of World War II.

Kenneth Kodson's *Away All Boats* was set aboard the U.S.S. *Belinda*, an American attack transport in the Pacific. Although not as stark as Monsarrat's *The Cruel Sea*, Kodson's novel was wider in its scope of action, with more meat on its bones, and was much more impressive as reading matter. *The Cruel Sea* made the better movie, however.

Another novel about the war in the Pacific, *The Big War* (1957), by a young author, Anton Myrer, was particularly perceptive and detailed in its descriptions. Myrer showed the degradations of the battlefield and the resulting brutalization and indifference, but he also showed gentleness and compassion. At times he worked hard to wring every last ounce of feeling out of a contrived situation. When some American soldiers came upon the body of a dead Japanese

woman, a geisha, on an island battlefield, Myrer wrote: "The idea of the corpse being the corpse of a woman, grenaded, her woman's entrails spilled in the harsh light of day, the soft fullness of her body faintly visible under the tight, quilted jacket, became a peculiar tribulation. It unnerved him subtly." "The soft fullness of her body faintly visible" was laying it on a bit thick. Corpses quickly become very bloated and burst out of their clothes, especially in the tropics, and one decomposing corpse looks much the same as any other.

Francis Juby Gwaltney was born in Traskwood, Arkansas, and served over three and a half years in the army in the Pacific. He received his B.A. and M.A. in Modern Literature from the University of Arkansas and for a time taught English. His novel *The Day the Century Ended* (1956) was about the coming to manhood of young Sam Gifford in the welter of blood of World War II. The book showed that American soldiers were not always noble heroes and good guys handing out chewing gum and candy bars to kids, and Gwaltney's humour could be black. For this he was attacked by some American reviewers. Gwaltney's characters differed from those of the bulldozer school of American war fiction exemplified in *The Naked and the Dead* and *Battle Cry*, being more distinguished for their mother wit than for their neuroses. One critic suggested that Gwaltney's characters had a conception of the values of civilized life, of leadership and chivalry. Perhaps, but it did not always show. Describing how some American soldiers found three Japanese bodies on the battlefield, Gwaltney was blunt:

> I stood guard while Willy searched them. Before he touched
> them, Willy thumped each of them solidly on the bridge of the

nose with a trench knife. Tusey uttered a grunt of elation when he found three gold teeth in the mouth of the first Jap he searched. He gleefully took a pair of rusted pliers from one of his cargo pockets and unceremoniously extracted his teeth, which he tenderly dropped into a Red Cross ditty bag, already heavy and bulging with wealth. He found another tooth in the second Jap.

One of the most remarkable books of World War II was written by the gifted Dan Billany who, had he survived the war, would undoubtedly have been a major writer in the fifties. Billany was killed in 1945; his novel *The Trap*, unrevised, was published in 1950.

Dan Billany was born in Hull in 1913 and after leaving school at the age fourteen became an errand boy and later an apprentice electrician. During the Great Depression of the thirties he was on the dole until it was docked by a Means Test committee. After vain attempts to earn a living he attended a local technical college and evening classes at the College of Commerce. He won a scholarship to Hull University, took an Honours English Degree in 1937, and became a teacher in Hull in the following year. In 1940 he joined the Army, and in June 1942 Lieutenant Billany was taken prisoner in North Africa and transferred to a P.O.W. camp in Italy. When the Italians capitulated in September 1943, he was liberated. Soon after the British P.O.W.s were released from the Italian camps, a former prisoner undertook to supply the Germans with information that would assist them in rounding up his own countrymen. While working to put an end to the activities of the odious informer, Billany was mortally wounded by him. He was buried near Ferro, not far from the Adriatic coast, in 1945.

Before and during the war he wrote several novels. The manuscripts of *The Trap*, written in Italian school exercise books, and *The Cage*, written on sheets of foolscap stitched together, were left in the care of a friendly Italian farmer who sent them to Billany's father after the war.

The Trap was a deeply moving book written with vigour, honesty, and compassion. An uncompromising young man related the story of his early years in Cornwall, of the girl with whom he fell in love, and the hard times endured by her family between the two wars. The narrative continued with a graphic account of life in the Army and the tensions and gruelling conditions in the Western Desert. In the last few lines of *The Trap* Billany wrote:

I do not hate the Italians, the Germans or the Japanese. I hate many of the things they have done.

The war emotions are frivolous. A grown man cannot take them seriously. The war is as ridiculous as Sweeney Todd, the Demon Barber. It is not related to the true feelings of real people.

Only the sufferings are real. The causes for which we suffer are contemptible and ridiculous.

Another articulate writer was New Zealander M. K. Joseph, a university lecturer in Auckland when his novel *I'll Soldier No More* was published in 1958. He had been at Oxford when the war broke out and then joined the Army. He served as an N.C.O. in the Field Artillery in an Air Observation Unit. His book was about a small group of privates and N.C.O.s in the invasion of 1944 and their slow advance through France and Belgium into Germany, and vividly conveyed their conversations and experiences. The boredom, the fear, the apathy about everything except what concerned them directly, and the sense of impending disaster, all had the ring of truth. People who had seen active service could recognize the reflection of their own experiences; and those who had not, realized immediately that, perhaps for the first time, they were learning what war was really like.

Tram-Stop by the Nile (1958) was by a new writer, Dave Wallis. The novel was set in wartime Egypt, when various small elements within the Allied Forces were beginning to work harder than ever with one eye cynically cocked toward their own future benefit, fiddling, flogging, and nest-feathering, while the sole war aim of most ordinary soldiers was to get home as fast as possible, no matter what. Dave Wallis was born in 1917, and lived in Canada. He had returned to England in 1935 and worked, among other things, as a labourer, a travel agency clerk, and a post office clerk until the outbreak of war. For six years he served in the Royal Corps of Signals and was in the Western Desert and other parts of the Middle East Command and finally in Germany. He knew his subject well.

Two excellent novels about the services both published in the fifties and written with a good deal of humour were *Idle on Parade* by William Camp and *The Bear Garden* by Michael Robson.

William Camp was born in Palestine and spent his childhood there. On leaving school in England he joined the Army and was sent to the Sixth Airborne Division, then stationed in Palestine. After a year he went to Oxford on an open scholarship to read Philosophy, Politics, and Economics, and then for a while he read for the bar. His book was about an unlikely recruit in a Guards regiment and how neither enjoyed the experience.

Much more penetrating was *The Bear Garden*, the story of Jake Hamilton and the R.A.F., to which he was called up to do his National Service. An eighteen-year-old individualist, Jake was not prepared to obey orders without question nor to suppress his opinions. The "Jakes" of the services, of which there were quite a few, had to learn a host of dodges and stratagems to retain their individuality, or let themselves be submerged in the tide of service bull and become mindless in order to survive.

James Kennaway was in his twenties when his first novel, *Tunes*

James Kennaway, author of
Tunes of Glory.

of Glory, was published in 1956. Born and educated in Scotland, he went to Oxford, where he edited an undergraduate paper. He served in the Cameron Highlanders and later worked as a reporter before joining the staff of a London publishing house.

Humorous and tragic, *Tunes of Glory* was set in the Scottish head-quarters of a Highland regiment, where Acting Colonel Jock Sinclair, D.S.O. and Bar, who had risen from the ranks and led his battalion in battle, was now mainly interested in seeing his officers scoff whisky and dance reels. With the arrival of a staff college and Whitehall trained colonel to take over from Jock, dissension began to grow as the new colonel attempted to force Sinclair and the battalion to conform to more conventional behaviour. There was comedy and pathos in the situations that arose and the tense battles of wills that led finally to tragedy. Once again a writer drew on his own experiences, in this case his service as an officer in a peacetime Scottish regiment. *Tunes of Glory* was full of the music of bagpipes and drums, martial, gay, and mournful.

One of the longest novels ever published in recent years was Mackinlay Kantor's *Andersonville*, which ran to 767 pages. It was awarded the Pulitzer Prize for fiction in 1956 and was described by the *New York Times* as the biggest fiction success since *Gone with the Wind*. A prolific author, Kantor nevertheless spent twenty-five years accumulating his research material for *Andersonville*, which was immediately acclaimed as the finest novel ever written about the American Civil War. Andersonville was the infamous stockade where thirty thousand Union troops were held prisoner by the Confederates in appalling conditions. The author concerned himself more with the people affected by the prison camp than with the camp itself, and in this fictionalized fragment of American history he plumbed the depths of human behaviour and showed that, heroic or vile, resolute or cowardly, bestial or noble, the psychology and behaviour of soldiers in war does not change.

Mackinlay Kantor was born in Webster City, Iowa, in 1904. He started to write seriously at the age of sixteen, was a newspaper reporter at seventeen, and an author devoted exclusively to fiction at the age of twenty-three. His first novel was published in 1928. Besides being prolific, Kantor was versatile, writing novels, collections of short stories, novelettes, verse, juvenile books, and histories. He wrote the original story that was made into the world-famous film *The Best Years of Our Lives*, which won thirteen Academy Awards. He spent eighteen months living the life of an ordinary patrolman in the New York City Police Department, had combat experience in two wars, and was personally decorated by the commander of the United States Air Force.

Following the success of his first novel, *The Blackboard Jungle*, Evan Hunter turned his spotlight on the jungle of the exurban American community. In *Strangers When We Meet*, the young husband is typical of the man who loves his wife and children yet seeks the stimulus of extra-marital relationships to relieve the monotony and pressures of the artificial society in which he lives. The feelings of guilt, and the problems, real and imagined, when he "does it on his own doorstep" by having an affair with the beautiful wife of his next-door neighbour, were the basis for Evan Hunter's novel.

In *A Matter of Conviction* Evan Hunter was concerned with modern society, disorder and law, crime and justice. His story was about the murder of a blind Puerto Rican by three teenage hoodlums in a New York slum. Henry Bell, assigned to prosecute the three boys, learned that justice, though blind, was not simple when he was beset on all sides by newspapers howling for the death penalty to be enforced as a deterrent to other gangsters; his neighbours, violently racialist when it came to Puerto Ricans, ostracizing him for prosecuting the Italian youths; and his superiors intent only on securing another conviction. But where did the blame really lie? As usual the question was asked what responsibility the parents bore for the guilt of their sons. Was the city itself guilty by allowing the existence of slums, where crime breeds and proliferates? And what about the solid citizens who, rather than see anyone suffer, shut their eyes? Hunter's literary style was strong and commanding, with an effective use of pungent and real dialogue and evocative and often disturbing descriptions.

Another best-selling American novel in 1958 was *Anatomy of a Murder* by Robert Traver, a brilliant dissection of a murder trial and all those involved. Writing with authority and great narrative skill, the author, once a public prosecutor and a high court judge himself, presented his story of a lawyer, Paul Biegler, involved in a murder trial. Biegler was persuaded by attractive Laura Manion to defend her husband – jailed for murdering Barney Quill, who she said had criminally assaulted her.

Biegler distrusted Laura and found her cold, egotistical husband, Army lieutenant Frederick Manion, objectionable, but he proceeded painstakingly with his enquiries into the case. In the climax, the trial itself, Traver brought vividly to life the relentlessness of the prosecutor, the sincerity of the knowledgeable judge, and the tensions and electric atmosphere of the courtroom. A film based on the novel was released in 1959.

Compulsion, by Meyer Levin, was a fictionalized true story based on the "intellectual" murder of the schoolboy son of a millionaire by two university students, Leopold and Loeb, also the sons of millionaires, a crime which had shaken American society in the thirties.

In a careful reconstruction of the case, the two academically brilliant, wealthy, and arrogant young men, with their homosexual relationship, and their immature ideas derived mainly from Nietzsche's philosophy of the superman, were well drawn. Levin also drew a well-delineated picture of the histrionics of the bravura defence lawyer, the Boanerges of the American criminal courts, mouthy Clarence Darrow, as well as recording the comprehensive, advanced, but typically

American author Evan Hunter, now better known as Ed McBain, the pen name under which he wrote the "87th Precinct" stories.

unconvincing psychiatric testimonies given at the trial. All combined to present a vivid, compassionate account of a social disaster, blamed, as usual, mainly on the parents of the criminals.

The subject of *Obsession* by Tom Gurr and H. H. Cox was perhaps even more horrible than that of *Compulsion*. It was the atrocious crime committed by two New Zealand schoolgirls in June 1954. Believing that the mother of one of them was trying to break up their lesbian relationship, they carefully plotted her murder with dispassionate thoroughness and at a prearranged time and place battered her to

64

Marilyn Monroe: a decade
in a face.

Liz Taylor and Michael
Wilding: love and
happiness, but for how
long?

death. Obviously influenced by Meyer Levin's *Compulsion*, Gurr and Cox used a punchy single-word title, and a similar approach, style, and treatment for *Obsession*. In endeavouring to unravel the complicated motivations of the two girls they interpreted established incidents and imagined incidents and conversations on their own terms. But they reported accurately details of the murder and the trial of the murderesses, even using the diary of one of the girls for intimate authenticities.

Far removed from psychological problems, Glendon Swarthout's theme for *They Came to Cordura* was heroism and cowardice. The novel was set in 1916 during the abortive American punitive expedition into Mexico. A middle-aged Awards officer of the campaign had been ordered to escort five U.S. cavalrymen cited for the Congressional Medal of Honor, and a young American woman prisoner suspected of treachery, to the U.S. military outpost at Cordura. On the arduous journey across rugged terrain the cavalrymen soon revealed their baser qualities, and Swarthout tried to show that heroism can emerge in a flash because of all sorts of reasons, including fear, from men who have few virtues, and that failure to display heroism at a particular time by a man of many virtues is not necessarily due to cowardice or a flaw in character.

A first novel published in 1958 was *The Sergeant* by the twenty-five-year-old American Dennis Murphy. A young American soldier at a post-war Army base in France is in love with a French girl, but his sergeant, homosexually attracted to him, tries to prise him away from her. The novel, though short, was well paced and dramatically written, but was limited in its reading appeal.

A successful formula novel with all the ingredients for a TV soap opera and reminiscent of *Peyton Place* was *The Bramble Bush* by Charles Mergendahl (1958). It was the usual account of sin, sex, and squabbles in a small New England town. The vague central theme was the problem of the morality of euthanasia facing a doctor whose friend, dying of an incurable illness, happened to have a beautiful wife to complicate the issue. Also there was a nurse in love with the doctor but who helped betray him; a blackmailing lawyer; the perverted editor of a local rag who got his jollies masturbating while taking nude pictures; the sick man's father, obsessed with hatred of the doctor's family; the town drunkard having an adulterous affair with the doctor's mother; and the good priest who brought the troubled doctor back to the Catholic faith. The book, with its ragbag of stock characters, was filmed in 1959 with Richard Burton, Barbara Rush, Jack Carson, and Angie Dickenson in her young days before she became a TV policewoman. The film was distasteful, but so was the book.

Lolita by Vladimir Nabokov, first published in America in 1955, was an entertaining but unsavoury story about a sophisticated, well-educated middle-aged man, Humbert Humbert, a lugubrious Central European, and his infatuation for a nubile schoolgirl. The prurient

Humbert's pathetic attempts to keep the interest of the precocious girl and to educate her, their sordid relationship as they traipsed all over America from one motel to another with him posing as the girl's father, could lead to no satisfactory result for the ill-assorted couple and culminated with Humbert, in the slough of despond, murdering his loathsome rival in a particularly gruesome manner.

Born in St. Petersburg in 1899, Nabokov went into exile in 1919. His first novels were written in Russian, but in 1940 he went to America and began to write in English. His writing, obviously influenced by James Joyce and T. S. Eliot, was rich with alliterations, French words, phrases, and sentences, literary references, and erudite allusions, and was a penetrating psycho-analytical study of unusual characters in extraordinary situations, some bordering on the pornographic. In 1959 when *Lolita* was published in Britain the Director of Public Prosecutions refrained from proceeding against the novel on the grounds of indecency, in spite of a good deal of clamour from articulate sections of the public.

Savagely humorous at times, sadistic, perverted, and outrageous at others, the narrative unfolded with Nabokov tilting sardonically at the American way of life with its motels, summer camps, and tourist traps, its educational system, its paper cup and Coca Cola economy, its consumer goods, and its society in general. "Nymphet", the word coined by Nabokov to mean a precocious, over-sexed school-girl, was quickly accepted in literary circles and passed into the English language.

Also by a Russian writer was *Doctor Zhivago*, the first major prose work by Boris Pasternak. Pasternak was born in Moscow in 1890; his father was a painter, his mother a musician. He studied law and music at Moscow University, became interested in philosophy, and went to Marburg in Germany, where he studied under Professor Cohen, returning to Russia shortly before the outbreak of war. He wrote many books of poetry and was regarded as the best Russian translator of the works of Shakespeare.

Doctor Zhivago was a rambling, often unconvincing account of a physician-poet caught up in the chaos of war and revolution, his flight from Moscow to take his wife and child to safety, and his passion for another woman, the beautiful Lara. It told of his peregrinations across the vast expanses of the Russian steppes as an unwilling member of a force of partisans and his gradual moral decline. Like so many Russian novels *Doctor Zhivago* was full of unbelievable coincidences and nostalgic memories, but it was distinguished by its lyrical descriptions of the Russian countryside.

In the fifties factual books about the war – biographies, memoirs, histories, documentaries, and dissertations, covering every branch of the armed services, civil services, and civilian populations of all Allied and Axis forces and all theatres of war, as well as translations of French and German war books – streamed into the book

66

Russian writer Boris
Pasternak.

market, swelling still further the gigantic mountain of war literature. There were excuses, whitewashes, recriminations, exposures, and some divulging of secrets. There were explanations, ifs and buts, and the wisdom of hindsight. There were remarkable revelations, and accounts of bravery and endurance and man's inhumanity to man. Millions of words; millions of pictures; billions of gallons of water under the bridge.

The Battle of France, 1940, first published in Britain in 1958, was a translation by A. R. P. Burgess of the book originally published in France under the title *1940; La Guerre des Occasions Perdues*. It was written by the French military historian Colonel A. Goutard, who had fought with the Free French forces, and the English version had a foreword by Captain Liddell Hart. Although the book was acclaimed in France by General de Gaulle and Marshall Juin, it was frigidly received by the French military authorities, who were not prepared to accept any explanation for the swift and overwhelming French defeat other than the ineptitude of the Government and the inferior equipment foisted on the military commanders. Goutard's attitude was that he sought the truth. His account of the French front's collapse in six days and the French Government's surrender less than six weeks after the start of Hitler's western offensive, and the operations of the British Expeditionary Force in Belgium and France, was a sweeping indictment of incompetent and lethargic military leaders; badly trained, badly treated, and ill-disciplined troops; and the insidious right-wing malaise that infected the whole body of France, causing apathy, despondency, and despair.

Peter Fleming was already an experienced author and writer when he wrote *Invasion 1940*, an account of German preparations for the invasion of Britain and Britain's counter-measures. Britain was fortunate in being able to rescue the B.E.F. from Dunkirk following Hitler's swift death blow at France. But Hitler had no intention of letting Britain off the hook. In his lively and comprehensive account of the dangers that threatened Britain in 1940, Fleming answered many questions that had puzzled the public. To do so he delved deeply into German as well as British archives and other sources. He gave details of elaborate German plans and their ruthless measures for the occupation of Britain, and put into strategical perspective the contrast between Hitler's dilatoriness in ordering Operation Sea Lion (the code name for the invasion) to be put into operation and his subsequent reluctance to abandon the venture even after the inherent flaws in the project had become all too plain. Also, in the light of new evidence, Fleming examined the strange delusions, the dogmas, and sanguine hopes, which underlaid Hitler's failure to maintain his initiative and annihilate Britain while the going was good.

Peter Fleming's next book, *The Siege at Peking* (1959), went back fifty-nine years to the time when the British, French, American, Japanese, and German legations in Peking were being besieged by the fanatical

Boxers and the Imperial Chinese Army. Fleming dug up plenty of new material to present a fascinating account of the strange siege where sandbags were made of silk, and pony steaks, strictly rationed, were washed down with unlimited bottles of champagne.

A definitive account of the great 1940 evacuation of the B.E.F. was David Divine's *The Nine Days of Dunkirk* (1959). Divine's account of the mounting of the massive operation to lift thousands of stranded British troops in mortal danger off the beaches around Dunkirk, the campaign leading to it, and the successful carrying out of the evacuation operations, was a sincere attempt to explode the myths and legends that surrounded what amounted to a colossal British defeat, and to put into focus the political climate and not public reactions at the time. According to Divine, great episodes of war attract legends, and Dunkirk, because of the magnitude of what was involved and the events leading to it, attracted more than its share. He tried to show that it was Gort, not Brooke, who extricated the small B.E.F. from the mess of the Dutch, Belgian, and French débâcle; and that contrary to its own claims, the R.A.F. did not win qualitative superiority over the Luftwaffe above the beaches. The book put into perspective such myths as the French opinion that Britain had abandoned France to its fate, and the belief that the B.E.F. had been saved only because Hitler stopped his Panzers on the An Canal and that King Leopold of the Belgians had betrayed the British Army. Divine also shattered the universal belief that the evacuation from the beaches was carried out by a vast fleet of heroic small craft spontaneously sailing out of English ports in an uncontrolled operation, when it was in fact a brilliantly conceived and infinitely flexible operation, planned, organized, and controlled by the genius of Admiral Ramsay from Dover.

In the fifties writers were pulling the wool of the war years from the public's eyes, and for the first time presenting facts and ideas hitherto hidden or obscured by propaganda, secrecy, whitewashing, and genuine security. For the first time, too, the public learned of units and operations of which they had until then been only vaguely aware.

Writers and men who had seen service in all sorts of units recounted their experiences or wrote of specialist services about which they had intimate knowledge, such as the Commandos, the Armoured Corps, and Airborne, and their books were widely read. For example, Hilary St. George Saunders, who had been a recorder with Lord Louis Mountbatten's Combined Operations H.Q., wrote *The Green Beret*, the story of the Commandos from 1940 to 1945, which was first published in October 1949. There had been fifteen impressions by May 1956, and in 1959 it was published as a paperback.

In 1950 Sir Bruce Lockhart, K.C., M.C., wrote *The Marines Were There*, a history of the Royal Marines in World War II. Brigadier Durnford Slater, D.S.O. and Bar, who had raised and led the first of the Commandos, Brigadier Derek Mills Roberts, C.B.E., D.S.O.,

M.C., and Murdoch McDougall followed with stories of their own particular Commandos.

Brazen Chariots by Robert Crisp, D.S.O., M.C., was another book about specialists by a specialist. It was an account of fighting in tanks in the desolate expanses of the Western Desert by a man who had fought in one. Bob Crisp had been a tank commander in the 3rd Royal Tank Regiment; before the war he had been a journalist and a fast bowler in the South African Test cricket team. His first-hand story, sharp, shocking, and revealing, but relieved by plenty of humour, was a unique account of a unique campaign.

R. W. Thompson was an author and journalist with extensive military experience. His assignments as a war correspondent had taken him through three wars, and as a soldier who had risen from the ranks to be a captain in the Army he had a deep understanding and feeling for men who had been under fire. His *Dieppe at Dawn* was the first complete account of the Dieppe raid, of the few crowded hours in August 1942 when in one of the costliest and most tragic operations in World War II a landing was made in the teeth of a relentless barrage from enemy batteries safely entrenched on the cliffs above. The assaulting force suffered over four thousand casualties, three-quarters of them Canadian, and lost over one hundred planes, over thirty ships, and forty armoured vehicles, without achieving any visible gain. Later it was claimed that the raid had provided valuable experience and lessons that contributed to the success of D-Day.

Thompson's previous book, *The Eighty-Five Days*, was about a later campaign, the battle fought by the Canadian First Army and the 52nd and 79th Divisions against the Germans fiercely resisting in the Breskens pocket, South Beveland, and the island of Walcheren. Thompson attempted to relate major strategy to the way it affected ordinary soldiers on the battlefield, but in *Battle for the Rhineland* (1958) he widened his scope, argued more controversially, and reassessed generalship forthrightly and realistically. "We were served by men, not Gods – or Sacred Cows", he wrote more in sorrow than in anger. Admitting that the generals had faced tasks of a greater magnitude than anything which had previously confronted human beings, he wrote that not one of them, in his view, was capable of commanding a group of armies. Even so, R. W. Thompson was being extraordinarily charitable.

C. E. Lucas Phillips had established his reputation as an author with his *Cockleshell Heroes*, the story of the attack by Royal Marine frogmen on enemy warships in occupied France, and *Escape of the Amethyst* about the incident in which a British gunboat had been involved on the Yangtse River in China in 1949. His book *The Greatest Raid of All* (1959) was an exciting and graphic account of the attack on St. Nazaire in occupied France in March 1942, when in a raid by "little ships", Royal Naval forces and Army commandos destroyed essential gear of the largest dockyard in the world to deny its use to the German Navy.

A different sort of raid, infinitely more devastating in its immediate effects, was the subject of a book by Walter Lord, a graduate of Princeton University and Yale Law School. Lord's reconstruction of the great *Titanic* disaster in *A Night to Remember* had scored a big success, and he applied a similar technique in his *Day of Infamy*, the story of the crushing Japanese attack on Pearl Harbor on December 7, 1942. The technique of interviewing hundreds of people personally connected with the event, both service personnel and civilians, was later used by Cornelius Ryan in *The Longest Day*; *The Last Battle*; and *A Bridge Too Far*.

Ken Attiwell, a Singapore veteran, used a similar technique in his account of the fall of Singapore in 1942, and answered a number of questions that had puzzled the public about the most inglorious defeat in British history. His book *The Singapore Story* also left many questions still unanswered, but it showed how muddle, incompetence, bloody-mindedness, and inept leadership led to the fall of Singapore and the subsequent Japanese occupation, and marked the end of the West's iron grip on the East.

In the closing months of the war, Fred Majdalany wrote his first novel, *The Monastery*, a short sketch of a part of the fierce struggle for Monte Cassino. Majdalany, born in 1913, had worked as a journalist, publicist, and B.B.C. writer, and until 1939 was drama critic of the *Sunday Referee*. During the war he fought in North Africa, Sicily, and Italy, was wounded and was awarded the Military Cross, and was later chief instructor at an Officer Cadets Training Unit.

His *Cassino, Portrait of a Battle* (1957) was a much more comprehensive book than his earlier work. Majdalany had taken part in the fighting as an infantry officer, and he made a detailed study of every phase and aspect of the operation from the highest strategic level down to the roles of individuals who had to sweat it out on the ground. He revisited the battlefield after the war and interviewed many people in the area who had been involved. His insight and perspicuity are apparent in his evaluation of the controversies surrounding the battle and the Allied bombing of the ancient Benedictine abbey which loomed menacingly over the Allied positions.

The Iron Curtain and the Cold War notwithstanding, the Russian struggle against the Germans in World War II, the epic battles around Kharkov, Leningrad, Moscow, Sebastapol, and Stalingrad, were tackled by authors with varying degrees of objectivity, hero-worship, grudging admiration, and bias. *Stalingrad . . . bis zur letzten Patrone*, published in an English translation in 1958, was by a typical German apologist, but Ronald Seth's *Stalingrad – Point of no Return* (1959) was written with an emphasis on Russian achievements. A former secret agent and author of *Secret Servants* and *The Lion with Blue Wings*, Seth told the story of Stalingrad from the Russian side, after an exhaustive study of German accounts of the battle, that shattered once and for all the myth of German military invincibility. Seth too, like Lord, Attiwell, and Ryan, fleshed out his book with dramatized stories gleaned from dozens of Russians who had taken part in the battle of blood and ice.

In the fifties a number of novels translated from the German were published in quick succession. Among them were *The Forsaken Army* by Heinrich Gerlach, *The Willing Flesh* and *The Savage Mountain* by Willi Heinrich, and *Other Men's Graves* by Peter Neumann.

Gerlach, who had been taken prisoner by the Russians at Stalingrad, claimed that he had collected the personal stories of hundreds of his fellow prisoners and used them as the basis for *The Forsaken Army*, which was told through the thoughts, conversations, and actions of many individuals. The result was that episodes, characters, and detailed descriptions seemed authentic enough even if the insight into the minds of German servicemen had been strained through a fine sieve before presentation.

Heinrich's *The Willing Flesh* was gratuitously advertised as achieving for the German Eastern Front in World War II what Remarque's *All Quiet on the Western Front* had done for the Western Front of World War I. It did nothing of the sort; Remarque's book was a classic. *The Savage Mountain* was a fanciful novel about three German N.C.O.s who stayed behind during a retreat to rescue a captured German general. The book, revealing and interesting, reflected Heinrich's experiences and reactions as a young corporal in a German infantry division on the Eastern Front, as well as later considerations and adjustments to fit in with contemporary thinking following the German defeat and the revelations of Nazi war crimes.

Two books about the invasion of Normandy, David Howarth's *Dawn of D-Day* and John Frayn Turner's *Invasion '44*, published in 1959, were not just military textbooks dealing with battles, operations, and the plots and plans of generals, and neither was Chester Wilmot's brilliant analysis *The Struggle for Europe*. Each was a well-considered account and each used a different approach in presenting its subject. Howarth tried to give an impression of the vast operation by concentrating on the experiences of a carefully selected cross section of men who had taken part in the campaign, instead of detailing units and giving exact descriptions of every isolated point of action. As a result, his account was an overall picture with plenty of impact, conveying in round terms what it was like for those who were there: the Airborne troops on the eve of D-Day, and those who swarmed ashore at dawn on June 6, 1944.

Turner, too, tried to give an overall picture by piecing together a good deal of information derived from authoritative accounts of specific aspects of the operations and the specialist units involved, by knowledgeable experts, analysts, and participants. Works consulted by Turner included *Above Us the Waves* by C. E. T. Warren and James Benson, for details of the vital piloting role of two midget submarines; *The Frogmen* by T. J. Waldron and James Gleason, for the work of the men who cleared beach obstacles; *The Marines Were There* by Sir Robert Bruce Lockhart, for information about the part played by the Commandos; *The Red Beret* by Hilary St. George Saunders, for the Airborne operations; *The Last Passage* by J. E. Taylor, for the part played by the old blockships; as well as dozens of other works for colourful snippets, vignettes, and eyewitness accounts to complete his picture.

An absorbing, authoritative, and most important book published in 1958 was *Arnhem* by R. E. Urquhart, C.B., D.S.O., Commander of the 1st Airborne Division which had borne the brunt of Operation Market Garden, Montgomery's plan for leap-frogging the Rhine by dropping at Arnhem in Holland. Urquhart related the story of the nine terrible days clearly, concisely, pungently, with some humour and little rancour.*

Another book by a former Airborne soldier was *Return Ticket* by Anthony Deane-Drummond (1953). This was a personal story by a man who had been captured in the first British parachute landing in Italy in 1941, had escaped after two attempts, and had joined the 1st Airborne Division to be dropped at Arnhem. After the remnants of the division had been evacuated and the battle was over, Deane-Drummond avoided capture by spending thirteen days hidden in a cupboard in a German guard-room, and then escaped once again. Like *The Wooden Horse* by Eric Williams, Deane-Drummond's was one of the spate of escape stories that captured popular imagination.

In 1951 appeared *Roger Keyes*, the well-balanced biography of Admiral of the Fleet Roger Keyes, G.C.B., K.C.V.O., C.M.G., D.S.O., by Brigadier-General Cecil Aspinall-Oglander who, during World War I, had been largely responsible for the successful management of the British evacuation from Gallipoli in 1915. Roger Keyes started his career in the fully rigged frigate *Raleigh*, and his life thereafter read like one long adventure story. He hunted slave traders, served on the Royal Yacht in the reign of Queen Victoria, took part in spectacular episodes in China during the Boxer rebellion, and in World War I his exploits became known all over the world: the Battle of the Bight, the Straits of Gallipoli, and the immortal raid on Zeebrugge. At the beginning of World War II he served as liaison officer with Leopold, King of the Belgians, and after the Belgian surrender energetically refuted accusations that Leopold had betrayed Britain, at a time when it was not popular or politically wise to defend scapegoats for the Continental débâcle of 1940.

Other biographies and memoirs published in the fifties included two long books by Arthur Bryant based on the diaries and auto-biographical notes of Field-Marshal the Viscount Alanbrooke, K.G., O.M., who had been adviser to Sir Winston Churchill. The first, *The Turn of the Tide, 1939–1943*, published in 1957, covered the period from the River Dyle to Dunkirk through to the Quadrant Conference at Quebec. Alanbrooke's diaries contained comments and details carefully styled for future publication. It was gratifying to learn from

*See my *Nostalgia—Spotlight on the Forties* (Jupiter Books, 1977).

them that the hoi-polloi in the field could be discussed in a civilized manner at a sherry party at Claridge's and that the King could chip in with comments; and that even in Russia, where the people were near starvation, big nobs and visiting firemen could be served breakfast consisting of caviare and food of every other description, including cake, chocolates, preserved fruit and grapes.

The Turn of the Tide covered the first eighteen months of Alanbrooke's term as Chairman of the Chiefs of Staff Committee. *Triumph in the West* covered his remaining three years as chairman and included the last two years of the war. It relied even more heavily on the Alanbrooke diaries than did the previous book.

Alanbrooke's carefully recorded assessments of the famous for posterity were perceptive and occasionally humorous. He stated that on more than one occasion he had to "tick off Monty", once for falling foul of both the King and the Secretary of State, and he had to "smooth off Monty's knack of making enemies". Another time, when dining with Monty at his H.Q., he had to tell him off and ask him not to meddle in everybody else's affairs, "such as wanting to advise Alex on his battle, or the War Office as to how to obtain reinforcements". Monty, it seemed, always remained unabashed.

The Memoirs of Field-Marshal Montgomery appeared in 1958 and were first and foremost an autobiography, every word of which had been written by the author, the first draft entirely in pencil. They covered the period of his early boyhood and service in World War I and the whole of his service throughout World War II, and there were many chapters devoted to post-war Europe and to the seven years in which Monty had served as Deputy Supreme Allied Commander in Europe. His criticisms of NATO, his sombre warnings of "insidious onslaughts of economic forces aimed at undermining the very foundations of our civilization", his dogmatic assertions, political utterances, and views of world events, were the puffings of an old general out of his element. Monty was in his element in World War II when his services, marred by one or two spectacular failures, were of incalculable value.

Defeat into Victory (1956) by Field-Marshal Sir William Slim purported to be the story of all the men who had fought in South-East Asia in World War II. Slim, with Admiral Mountbatten as Supremo backing him, was able to organize his newly formed Fourteenth Army made up of British, Indian, and African divisions into a formidable force in the China-Burma-India theatre of war and to smash Japan's legendary invincibility in jungle warfare.

The book was a record of a major campaign that ranged over a thousand miles of territory from the advance of the Japanese into India, the destruction of the Japanese divisions at the battle of Imphal-Kohima; the Allied advance on the Central Front across the Chindwin, across the Irrawaddy to destroy the Japanese forces grouped around Mandalay; the attack on Meiktila; and the two-pronged race against time to reach Rangoon before the monsoons bogged down troops and transports. In his lucid account of the operations, Slim adopted a mostly detached and modest style, giving credit where he thought it was due both inside and outside of his command. He was generally understanding in his assessments and opinions of controversial figures such as "Vinegar Joe" Stilwell, though he was possibly somewhat prejudiced against Wingate.

Orde Wingate by Christopher Sykes was published in 1959. Sykes was well qualified to write the biography of Wingate, who was a military genius, a scholar, and one of the most unusual and outstanding figures of World War II. Sykes himself was born in 1907 and educated at Downside, Christ Church College, Oxford, and the Sorbonne. After serving as a junior official in the British Embassy in Teheran, he studied at the School of Oriental Studies and returned to Persia and Afghanistan in 1933 to study the campaigns of the 1914–18 War in the Persian interior and Central Asia. During World War II he served in G.H.Q. Middle East, Cairo, in Persia, and in Palestine, and then in the Special Air Service. He was awarded the Croix de Guerre and was mentioned in dispatches.

In his well-written and well-researched account, he traced Wingate's ancestry, his deeply religious and bookish youth, his schooldays, and his travels in the Middle East, and also his military background and the first signs of military prowess in the organization of special patrols against Arab terrorists in Palestine. Wingate was passionately vocal and practical in his support of the Jews in their struggle for a Jewish State.

During the war Wingate commanded troops in the immediate service of Haile Selassie, the Ethiopian emperor, and his brilliant campaign of bluff played a notable part in defeating the Italians in Ethiopia and restoring the emperor to his throne. But it is as leader of the Chindits that Wingate is probably best remembered, when he led his independent brigade far behind the Japanese lines in Burma, harassing communications and depots. Sykes refuted criticisms of Wingate's policies, arguing convincingly that Wingate's two Chindit expeditions paid handsome dividends in gnawing away at the Japanese vitals and paving the way to the complete crushing in the field of the much-vaunted Imperial Japanese Army.

Another hard look at the struggle against the Japanese octopus was *Retreat from Kokoda* by Raymond Paull (1959). Paull's masterly account told of half-trained, poorly equipped Australian troops, outnumbered four to one by crack Japanese troops, fighting along the Kokoda Trail in New Guinea, and how their courage and endurance in a jungle hell sowed the seeds of Australian victory. Paull's detailed and well-authenticated story brought into sharp focus a cruel campaign little known outside Australia, and he did not pull his punches as he chronicled the mistakes, procrastinations, and ineptitude of the authorities and the disastrous consequences for the unlucky men who had to fight.

Many books about the war in the Western Desert, including several about Rommel, were written in the fifties. Brigadier Desmond Young, a veteran of World War I, served under Field-Marshal Sir Claude Auchinleck, and when he was captured at Gazala in the Western Desert, had been saved from German harassment by the personal intervention of a German general, unmistakably Rommel. Later Young escaped from his captors. His biography *Rommel*, published in 1950, was a crisp, well-delineated, and sensitive account of a flamboyant leader of men in the field. Young had dug deeply to unearth relevant documents and records and had interviewed scores of people, including Rommel's widow and son, in order to present Rommel the man and soldier. In so doing he revealed a rare and remarkable German.

The Foxes of the Desert was a translation by Mervyn Savill of the novel by Paul Carrel originally published in Germany under the title *Die Wüstenfüchse* in 1958. Carrel was a well-known journalist who had served with the German Foreign Office during the Nazi régime and had become an Intelligence officer. It was a history from the German side of the Afrika Korps from its arrival in North Africa in 1941 to its final surrender in 1943. Written more or less objectively, it lost nothing in the excellent English translation and made fascinating reading.

Two books by Lord Russell of Liverpool castigated the Germans and the Japanese for their behaviour in the years preceding World War II and during the war itself. *The Scourge of the Swastika* was a short history of Nazi war crimes, *The Knights of Bushido* a short history of Japanese war crimes.

The Scourge of the Swastika was not just an indictment of German atrocities and bestialities, but a factual account·written without passion and told objectively. There was no attempt at sensationalism, and the moderate tone and the almost low-key approach made the chronicle of the appalling events even more chilling.

The Knights of Bushido was written twelve years after the end of the war, at a time when the torture and degradation inflicted by the Japanese on their captives had already been largely forgotten, except by the survivors. The book was a report, with no suggestion of exaggeration, of fully documented records of Japanese atrocities given in evidence at trials for war crimes.

The war in Korea, which started in June 1950 and ended in July 1953, could have been on the moon for all most people in Europe and America cared. They had had enough of their own war, and provided none of their own were unlucky enough to be forced to fight in Korea, they ignored the war there.

Reginald Thompson's *Cry Korea* was published in 1952, *Korean Tales* by Melvyn B. Vorhees appeared in 1953, and *Substitute for Victory* by John Dill in 1954; but an outstanding novel of the war nobody wanted to hear about was *The Dead, the Dying and the Damned* by D. J. Hollands.

Wingate inspects a soldier
of the Ethiopian Battalion,
Dambacha, April 1941.

Douglas John Hollands had as a National Serviceman served as
an infantry platoon officer with the 1st Battalion, the Duke of
Wellington's Regiment in Korea from October 1952 until August
1955. He was awarded the M.C. for patrol actions at the age of twenty
and later was on the staff of the Commonwealth Forces H.Q., Japan.
His novel was a gripping story of National Servicemen, youngsters
between the ages of eighteen and twenty, who were sent to fight in
a war they neither understood nor wanted to understand, in a country
most of them had never even heard of, and where they were sure
they had no business. They greeted with a hollow laugh the high-flown

assertions that the war was a United Nations fight for the defence of liberty. The only freedom they wanted was their own, to get home and out of uniform.

Hollands struck the right note in his fictionalized true story, and showed that even men dragooned into fighting an unpopular war, or being used to make futile political gestures, can show courage and fortitude as they did in Palestine and Malaya.

They fly through the air

WAY BACK IN 1955 I WAS DISCUSSING FLYING SAUCERS WITH MY good friend and neighbour Earl Beaver, a jet pilot in the U.S. Air Force who had flown Sabre jets in Korea. Earl did not claim to have seen a saucer of the type so often described in the Press, but he believed that they were experimental aircraft being developed in secret by the United States, Russia, Britain, and France. He thought a flying saucer might be some sort of jet-powered gyroscopic discus, possibly operated by remote control, and that it could be made to hover, accelerate, and manoeuvre at ultra-supersonic speeds. It could probably carry camera equipment for reconnaissance, or could carry conventional explosives or nuclear devices in the same way as a rocket weapon. Earl believed that people who claimed to have seen saucer-like craft had either exaggerated their performance or had overestimated their speed and manoeuvrability. The chances are he was right and that like many other experimental aircraft and rockets, saucers were abandoned or were superseded by other developments which made the saucer idea obsolete. It was probably the development of earth satellites that ended the saucer experiments.

In 1960, a V.T.O.L. aircraft, the Avro VZ-9V Avrocar, made its appearance. Such an aircraft, seen flying around in the early experimental stages, could well have given rise to a good many saucer stories. The craft had three Continental J69 engines to drive a central fan providing a peripheral air curtain and ground cushion for V.T.O.L. operation.

It seems certain, however, that not everyone who claimed to have seen a flying saucer actually saw one of the experimental aircraft. Imagination plus brainwashing by Press, radio, and television could have made saucers out of conventional aircraft, meteorites, sky reflections, or some sort of atmospheric ignis fatuus, or even patches of St. Elmo's fire playing around ordinary aircraft. Others claiming to have seen saucers were possibly jumping on the bandwagon as people are prone to do in order to pick up a little notoriety: or they could have just been people whose imaginations had been playing them tricks. Reports on saucers described them variously as being round, cigar-shaped, or disc-like. Such descriptions were not really contradictory. It could depend on the view of the flying object. The side view would be cigar-like, the underside would appear circular, and a banking saucer would be like an elliptical disc. With jets all round the perimeter, the flames from the exhausts would appear as a glow when spinning and as lights when hovering motionless.

A friend of mine told me he had actually had a long look at a flying saucer whilst on holiday in Dorset. He had made some drawings of it which he later showed me. But as my friend was a highly imaginative strip cartoonist who specialized in stories about space travel and whose drawings of spaceships and rockets were always detailed and authentic-looking, he could have dreamt the incident. Or perhaps he was just putting me on.

Of course, it is possible that flying saucers do come from outer space. Earthmen have landed on the Moon and have sent machines to explore Mars and Venus. If there are beings living on the Moon and Mars they could send their ships to Earth. Indeed, if there are highly intelligent creatures living in deep space it is feasible that they could be probing Earth. Perhaps they wish to settle here. Perhaps after their long series of reconnaissances they have decided that there must be far better places on which to live than our own troubled planet. And nobody can argue against that.

During World War II there were reports from Allied airmen that they had sighted strange round glowing objects in the skies over Europe and the Far East. Sometimes the objects, which they called "foo-fighters" or "Kraut fireballs", appeared singly and sometimes in formation, hovering, darting, or travelling at high speed. After the war the information was checked with the enemy by Intelligence officers to ascertain whether the objects had been some secret enemy weapon, but that was discounted when it was found that both German and Japanese pilots had also been baffled by the mysterious flying objects.

In May 1946 there were reports of a sighting of a mysterious flying object in America, and very soon reports were coming in from all over the world that these strange objects had been seen streaking across the sky. The usual explanations advanced by the authorities and the Press were that the sightings had been optical illusions or natural phenomena.

In June 1947, Kenneth Arnold, an American business man from Idaho, claimed that while flying in a private plane near Mount Rainier, Washington, he had seen a formation of nine huge discs, each of which he estimated measured at least a hundred feet across and was travelling at over a thousand miles an hour. Arnold described them as being like "flying saucers" – and the name stuck. Soon hundreds of reports of "flying saucers" were coming in from all over America. The United States Air Force Intelligence investi-

Barbara Goalen: fashion-modelling acceptable to the upper classes.

1950s leisure fashion: never
mind the appearance, look
at the chest *support*.

gating the stories referred to the mysterious aircraft officially as un-identified flying objects (U.F.O.s).

Many detailed stories of encounters with U.F.O.s by U.S. Air Force personnel and civilians from all walks of life appeared in the Press, and there were also interviews on radio and television. It was soon being widely suggested by pundits, scaremongers, and know-alls that the saucers emanated possibly from Mars or Venus but most likely from a planet outside our own solar system where there existed intelligent life far in advance of our own.

Knowledgeable pronouncements by scientists, pseudo-scientists, sci-fi writers, Press-wise reporters, and correspondents embellished the tales, plausible or otherwise, of saucer sightings, and it was darkly hinted that the authorities were deliberately playing down the problem or were involved in some big cover-up conspiracy in order not to provoke panic among the public. Items in the Press reminded people how, in 1939, Orson Welles' New York broadcast of *The War of the Worlds* had scared listeners out of their wits and had sent them scurrying hither and thither in the belief that Martians had invaded Earth and were knocking ten skittles of hell out of Earth's military forces.

After the excitement of World War II, the immediate post-war period was an anticlimax, and a saucer story could make good copy for news hungry writers, especially when it could be slanted with an anti-Russian angle in the hotting-up Cold War. Was the flying saucer a new Russian weapon? Were saucers Russian rockets? More people thought that more likely than theories of intruders from Mars or another planet, especially the cynical or those who remembered the Welles broadcast.

Nevertheless the U.S. Air Force continued to check out every U.F.O. report from their personnel and tried to find logical explanations. It was suggested in some quarters that in one particular instance the U.F.O. sighted had been the planet Venus; other sightings had been meteorological balloons, meteorites, American experimental missiles, and even birds. The U.S. services were upset when the media publi-cized explanations that U.F.O.s were secret U.S. weapons or a new design of jet-propelled Navy plane, and the White House joined the services in emphatically denying such stories. But a lot of the public did not believe the denials.

From January 1950 reports of U.F.O. sightings came in regularly from all over the United States. According to the Press, on February 1, 1950, thousands of people in Tucson, Arizona, had seen a mysterious object shoot over the city, slow down, then hover for a moment before streaking off to the west trailing a long tail of black smoke. A few weeks later, U.S. Navy radar men tracked two glowing U.F.O.s seen over Key West and calculated that they were flying fifty miles above the ground. Soon afterwards, an officer of the Chilean Navy, Commander Augusto Orrego, reported from his Arctic base that on a clear night he and his men had observed several saucers flying one above the other, manoeuvring at tremendously high speeds. Photographs were said to have been taken, but if that was so none of the photographs were shown to the public.

Again from all parts of the world, Mexico, Cuba, Peru, Turkey, and other countries, there came reports of sightings of weird disc-shaped metallic flying objects, but there were no claims that any of them had been photographed. On March 9, over Dayton, Ohio, a saucer was spotted and four fighter planes were scrambled to intercept it, but by the time they reached the vicinity of the alleged sighting the quarry had vanished.

On March 21, two American pilots of Chicago and Southern Airlines flying a DC-3 plane from Memphis, Tennessee, to Little Rock, Arkansas, saw a peculiar bluish-white glare in the night sky between Lonoke and Stuttgart. As the object approached the plane, the men saw that it was a saucer-like machine with a double row of bluish lights along its length which they assumed to be lighted port-holes. The machine circled their plane, then suddenly zoomed away at incredible speed.

At about the same time a commander in the U.S. Navy who was also a rocket expert published an article about three sightings near the White Sands guided missile base. One large saucer flying at an estimated speed of eighteen thousand miles an hour fifty-six miles above the earth was probably a rocket, a forerunner of Earth satellites. Two smaller discs, tracked from five observation posts and seen to pace an Army high altitude rocket, were probably reflections of the rocket, although it was said that the discs speeded up and soon out-distanced the rocket. Most likely the discs were reflections of the rocket and as the rocket climbed higher into the sky these reflections appeared higher and higher above it until they disappeared as the rocket was no longer reflected.

In June above Hamilton Field, California, an unidentified flying machine trailing what appeared to be grey-green exhaust made three passes at an estimated speed of more than a thousand miles an hour over the field's control tower. The speed could have been grossly exaggerated, of course, and the machine could have been flown by some joker. But even in the fifties speeds of a thousand miles an hour could have been made by experimental planes.

In July a most unlikely story accompanied by two smudgy photographs of a flying circle was printed by a small weekly publication and started a whole new crop of rumours and speculations. The first picture was of a large disc tilted at an angle. The caption stated that the object, hit by flak rockets, had exploded in a shower of fireworks and that about twenty silvery capsules had floated to the ground. The second picture showed a weird shining figure about three feet tall held by the arms by two C.I.A. types in trench-coats while two girls looked on in amazement. The caption for this picture stated that as one of the capsules broke open the first Martian man was captured and that an eyewitness, a Texas G-man, had by chance been

s easy to see how the
rocar experimental
craft could have been
staken for a flying saucer.

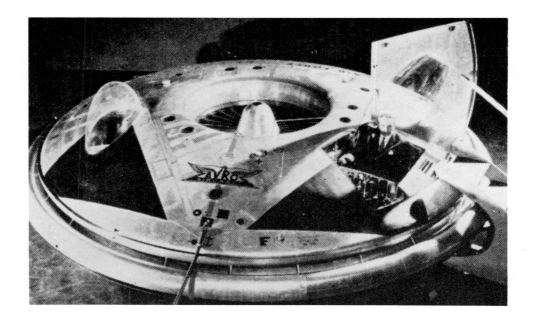

on the spot. The story was not new, however. A similar story had appeared before – first in *Variety*, and later in *Behind the Flying Saucers* by Frank Sculley.

By now all flying saucer stories, even those from apparently reliable sources, were being met with scepticism if not ridicule, and it was said that pilots of service and civilian planes were reluctant to report any U.F.O. they saw or thought they saw. But there were still pilots who, claiming to believe what they thought to be the evidence of their own eyes, filed reports of their sightings despite Air Force disclaimers, public scepticism, and the hot-and-cold attitude of the Press.

On January 20, 1951, the control tower at Sioux City Airport asked Lawrence W. Vinther, a captain of Mid-Continental Airlines flying a DC-3, to check out a strange glowing object above the field. As Vinther tried to approach the object it suddenly dived on his plane, reversed abruptly, then flew alongside the DC-3 for several seconds. Vinther and his co-pilot described the object as being larger than a B-29 with no visible means of propulsion. Both men were vehement in their insistence that what they had seen was, as far as they were concerned, no known or explainable means of air transport.

According to Dr. Liddel of the American Office of Naval Research, saucers were the Navy's cosmic-ray research balloons known as "sky-hook", giant gas-filled plastic bags which often rose to 100,000 feet. He implied that all other explanations were from Cloud-cuckoo-land. A former U.S. Air Force scientist, Dr. Anthony O. Mirachi, would have none of this. In his opinion the Navy report was a sop for a worried public. Mirachi thought the saucers might be experimental rockets of a potential enemy (meaning Russia) and should be investigated to avert what could turn out to be a more devastating disaster than Pearl Harbor.

83

But there was an abundance of evidence that could be used to shoot down the already leaky balloon theory, although it was admitted that balloons could have accounted for perhaps 20 per cent of the sightings. Mirachi's warning was unnecessary as the Air Force was already well aware of the possibility that the saucers were experimental missiles or flying machines of a foreign power and had been investigating along those lines using specially trained scientists and analysts.

In the first few months of 1951 there were few U.F.O. reports in the Press. The war in Korea, proving to be a bigger headache than the Americans had bargained for, was going badly as the Chinese allies of the North Koreans launched offensive after offensive. There were more than enough headlines for the American Press without having to dish up U.F.O.s to boost circulations. But with the beginning of truce talks at Kaesong in July, it was time to give Korea a rest and to turn to the latest news on the U.F.O. front.

On July 14 it was reported that two radar operators in the United States had seen an object on their scope which appeared to be moving very fast, and at the same time a tracker observing a B-29 bomber through binoculars saw what appeared to be a large U.F.O. flying very close to it. Another observer, with a 35mm camera, managed to take two hundred feet of film of the object, but because of its high altitude all that showed on the reel was a round bright spot — which was taken to be proof enough.

While flying over New Jersey on September 11, an Air Force jet pilot caught sight of a gleaming disc flying at an estimated speed of nine hundred miles an hour. Once again an experimental plane could have accounted for the sighting. Even a conventional jet-fighter seen for just a second or two from another jet could appear to be a gleaming disc. On September 14 at Los Alamos another U.F.O. was seen in the vicinity of the Atomic Energy Laboratory, not the first time saucers were reported over atomic stations. On September 23, two F-86 jets were sent up from March Field, California, to investigate a U.F.O. Guided by Ground Control Intercept, the pilots spotted a round silver object flying at approximately fifty thousand feet. The strange machine circled above the jets, and although four more jets were scrambled, none were able to reach the altitude of the U.F.O. and the frustrated pilots were unable to add anything new to what was already known about U.F.O.s.

What project analysts considered to be an extremely important sighting was made on October 11 by J. J. Kalizewski, a scientist working on the Navy cosmic-ray study at Minneapolis, and a General Mills–Navy balloon project engineer flying as observer in a plane checking a cosmic-ray research balloon. Suddenly they saw a gleaming object streak past at terrific speed. It checked speed for a moment as it crossed above and ahead of their plane, circled, then with astonishing acceleration it turned away and disappeared into the distance. A minute or two later that or a similar object appeared as from nowhere.

It moved so rapidly that Kalizewski was unable to track it, but from
the ground the machine was seen briefly through a theodolite telescope
by a technician at the airport. The witnesses told an Intelligence officer
called in to investigate the sighting that in their opinion the machine
had been under control. The experienced Kalizewski maintained that,
whatever the objects were, of one thing he was certain: what he had
seen was nothing like anything he had ever seen before. In his opinion
the Government should immediately order a twenty-four-hour alert.

Air Force Intelligence had in fact already initiated work on such
a plan. Two hundred special grid cameras capable of revealing
whether the glow of a U.F.O. was caused by radiant heat, exhaust
trail, or by some other source of power and light, were set up.
It was also planned to use cine-theodolites similar to those used
to photograph guided missiles, as their progress was tracked, as
well as specially adapted sonar sound-detection devices able to pick
up the faintest sound of any form of propulsion.

At the beginning of 1952 there was a drop in the number of reported
sightings in the United States, but from Canada came a detailed report
of a U.F.O. sighting over a Royal Canadian Air Force jet base in
North Bay. A disc glowing orange-red had appeared at a high altitude,
and for eight minutes it was observed diving, circling, and zig-zagging
at supersonic speeds in the stratosphere. It was estimated to be one
of the largest U.F.O.s ever reported.

A second sighting over North Bay was reported some little time
later, and the R.C.A.F. Intelligence began to sit up and take notice.

85

A formation of orange-red discs had been seen high above Toronto moving at high speed, and on May 1 a saucer was sighted as it flashed over Ottawa at an estimated speed of thirty-six hundred miles per hour.

British newspapers too were making capital of home-bred saucer sightings. In January 1952, reports came from a farm near Canterbury, Kent, that a golden object with flames shooting from its nose was seen travelling at a great height. This was something different. Instead of the usual silver this was gold; instead of flames coming out of the tail, flames came from the nose. The eyewitness, an ex-W.A.A.F. officer, said in an interview in the *Sunday Dispatch* (April 20, 1952) that what she had seen was definitely not an aeroplane. (And it had definitely not been an airborne Crocodile tank either.)

In February a nineteen-year-old undergraduate at Jesus College, Cambridge, claimed that he had seen from the college grounds a bright round object travelling high in the sky and that he was able to observe it for fifteen seconds. He said it had a perfectly rounded surface in the centre of which was a particularly bright spot of light. There was no corroboration for this story. It could have been the result of a jolly party.

In May a U.F.O. was reported over Canterbury, then Aldershot, Poole, and Southampton. According to the Press it had been seen by a number of people in the south-west. It was described as a metallic disc-shaped object with a bright surface reflecting the sunlight. The description appeared in an article in the *Sunday Dispatch* of June 1. About seven weeks later the *Daily Worker* reported a U.F.O. sighting, this time, naturally enough, by a working-class chap, a motor mechanic, and his wife, at Ashton-under-Lyne, Lancashire. The U.F.O. was described as a large circular object like a parachute which flew off at high speed towards Stalybridge.

In the States none other than the Navy Secretary, Dan Kimball, was involved in a flying saucer incident while flying to Hawaii. He vouched for the fact that his plane had been buzzed by a U.F.O. Perhaps it was just a gremlin. Not long after this came a report from New Mexico that an Air Force instructor had sighted a shiny oval-shaped machine flying at an extremely high altitude. It was estimated that the machine was at least six times larger than a B-29. From Norway came a story of a bluish-coloured light above an electric power plant, which resolved into a glowing disc shape as it descended, and a few days later it was stated that hundreds of people in Singapore had seen an unidentified rocket streaking across the sky. No doubt many of them hastily resorted to Tiger Balm to steady their nerves.

Newspapers and magazines were having a field day with U.F.O. stories, some seriously suggesting that the mysterious flying objects came from outer space and that the ordinary man in the street was very worried. Actually very few people took the hocus-pocus seriously, or indeed were interested in the subject at all. Speculation about the existence, the source, and the purpose of flying saucers appealed mainly to the small section of the public who were sci-fi buffs. To try to drum up more interest from the bored general public, the Press published articles suggesting that the authorities took a serious view of the threat posed by U.F.O.s. For their part the authorities were not very pleased to read that. Accordingly they played down U.F.O. stories and offered what seemed to be reasonable and logical explanations for most of them, discounting the rest as being too vague to bother about.

In June 1952 radar men from Goose Bay Air Force Base in Labrador picked up the track of a U.F.O. and a strange machine with red lights became visible over the field. It was seen to pulsate, turn white, and then accelerate away. The suggestion was that the sudden application of power had caused more heat and hence the change in colour.

During the first week or two in July saucer sightings were being reported from all over the world, flying singly, in pairs, and in groups. In the United States, defence bases, atomic plants, and military planes were said to be the main targets of the saucer operators, whoever they were, and the Midwest States were thought to be under special surveillance for some reason that could not be conjectured.

On July 5 a number of pilots reported seeing a flying saucer over the atomic energy plant at Richlands, Washington, and a news dispatch from Korea, where the war was in the doldrums and President Rhee's latest antics were not considered newsworthy, described a sighting of two U.F.O.s by Canadian naval officers. It seemed that for over an hour they had watched the saucers darting around above their ship. Whether what the Canadians had seen was an apparition akin to the Angel of Mons, or was the result of boredom or a little too much Navy rum, or whether it was a contrived story to supplement the paucity of hard news coming out of Korea, was not important. What the Navy men witnessed may have been an ordinary dogfight between Migs and Sabre jets. Meanwhile, U.S. Navy Intelligence was hard pressed trying to sift through the information of new sightings from various parts of the United States.

On July 12 news came from the Midwest that at one o'clock that night a saucer glowing blue-white (the latest colour for saucers) had streaked over Indiana, and at Delphi it was seen by a number of civilians including a former Air Force jet pilot working as a flight test analyst for the Northrop Aircraft Company. For once the story did not make the newspapers. However, the following night, Saturday, when the streets and parks were thronged with people, a bright yellow glow appeared in the sky and onlookers were amazed to see an oval machine trailing flaming exhaust shoot across the city at a height of no more than five thousand feet. Within minutes switchboards at police stations and newspaper offices and at the airport were jammed with calls from puzzled, curious, and scared citizens. Accounts of the sightings were passed by word of mouth, growing more weird, detailed, and scary at each telling. As the U.F.O. was approaching

It's not difficult to fake a
flying-saucer photograph.

88

Indianapolis it had been seen by several airline pilots, one of whom, flying an American Airlines Corvair, had first spotted it when he was about thirty miles south-east of the city flying at five thousand feet and travelling at three hundred miles an hour. He estimated that the saucer was at roughly fifteen thousand feet and was moving at least three times as fast as the plane. It dropped to the level of the Corvair then took off towards the city. A similar story was told by five other pilots, all of them level-headed and reliable. Radar men who had picked up the machine on their screens earlier computed its speed at some seventeen hundred miles per hour and estimated that it was as large as a B-36 bomber.

On the same night a Pan-American DC-4 was nearing Norfolk, Virginia, en route to Miami, cruising at eight thousand feet, when the pilot saw six huge discs, glowing orange, approaching at high speed below his craft, in echelon. Suddenly the leading disc canted and changed course and the others followed suit. Two more flying saucers flew beneath the DC-4 and accelerated to catch up with the formation. Twelve hours later, near Newport News, a commercial flyer saw two saucers travelling at an estimated speed of more than six hundred miles an hour. Another saucer was seen by a naval officer at Miami, and there were also sightings at Norfolk, the Bahamas, and Hampton, Virginia.

On July 17, 1952, the captain of an American Airlines DC-6 received a warning from a flight ahead that a formation of U.F.O.s had been sighted. He and his crew peered into the sky and suddenly saw four lights flash by at an estimated speed of three thousand miles per hour. The next day the newspapers carried the story and in addition a story from Veronica in Argentina where six unidentified machines had circled in full view of the residents a few hours after the DC-6 sighting.

Newspaper and public speculation about the mysterious flying objects flared up once again. As usual, some sightings were explained, others discounted, and a few remained a mystery. Once more it was stated that flying saucers were coming from outer space for the purpose of reconnoitring the earth, surveying, recording, planning, perhaps with peaceful intentions but perhaps not.

At the end of June, according to an account published in the *Saarbrücken Zeitung*, six Norwegian jet fighters flying near Hinlopen Straits, between North East Land and Spitzbergen, were surprised when their radios suddenly jammed. Circling the area near Spitzbergen trying to locate the possible cause, the crews saw a metallic object on the snow below. They immediately reported their discovery, and a Norwegian Air Force officer and a rocket expert were sent to investigate. They landed in ski planes and examined the object, which was a disc measuring some 125 feet in diameter and containing a complex of remote-control radio units which were thought to have caused the radio interference. The saucer-like machine was powered by forty-six jets on the outer rim which would cause an inner ring to

Could this have been a U.F.O.? It is a tilt-wing V.T.O.L. aircraft built for the U.S. army in 1956.

rotate when they were in operation. The whole contrivance was dismantled and shipped to Narvik for further examination. Instruments on the saucer bore Russian markings, and, according to the *Zeitung*, experts estimated that the machine had a flight range of eighteen thousand miles, could reach an altitude of a hundred miles, and was equipped to carry explosives, nuclear or conventional. Although all knowledge of the disc was denied by the Norwegian Government for obvious reasons, that particular saucer could well have been a Soviet machine of advanced design similar to the Avro VZ-9V Avrocar V.T.O.L. aircraft.

On the night of July 20 radar men at the Air Traffic Control Center in Washington were amazed when their scopes suddenly recorded a series of sharp blips indicating aircraft. It was evident from the strange behaviour of the blips that these were not ordinary aircraft, and for five hours they circled and manoeuvred over Washington, sometimes flying at low speeds and at other times accelerating in seconds to speeds of seventy-two hundred miles per hour. A man claimed that he had seen five gigantic discs circling above the city. The men in the control tower were severely shaken by the night's events. So were Air Force and Military Intelligence which had been notified. If anybody in Intelligence knew what had been going on, nothing was told to the public. All the same, people got wind of the strange Washington phenomenon and wanted to know what it was all about.

People in Texas, California, New Jersey, and dozens of other places all over the United States claimed that they had seen flying saucers. A claim to have seen one was a sort of status symbol. On the night of July 23, Boston and the West Coast had their own mysterious visitors. Some engineers who saw them were sure they were manned or under remote control, and other eyewitnesses expressed their opinion that they were secret U.S. Air Force weapons.

An article in a London Sunday paper said that a fifty-foot metallic disc had been seen in a forest clearing near Hasselbach, Germany,

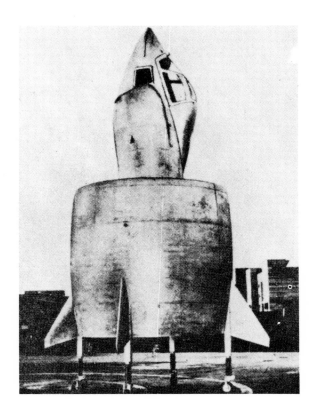

An even odder-looking aircraft – a French jet-powered V.T.O.L. of 1956.

in the Soviet zone. Two men in shiny protective clothing had been seen to enter it through what appeared to be a retractable conning-tower. Then the outer rim of the machine had grown red as the ring rotated, and the saucer rose spinning like a top. There is no reason why the report should not have been true. It could have been a type of V.T.O.L. device like the Avrocar or a flying platform for use in reconnaissance. If it was true it gave credence to the Spitzbergen discovery. On the other hand it could have been a tale based on that report in the *Saarbrücken Zeitung*. Whatever it was, it put the breeze up the Pentagon and lots of people who thought the Russians could be preparing to pounce (according to the news-papers, which as usual were using U.F.O.s as a useful running story).

The next U.F.O. report was from Culver City, where it was said that several workers at an aircraft plant had seen a silver craft described as elliptical in shape and flying over the city with a rocky motion at a high altitude. At one time it had hovered, and two small discs were seen to be launched from the starboard side (whichever side that is on a flying saucer). The smaller saucers had cruised around the city for a while and were then taken back aboard the mother craft.

On the night of July 26 the Naval Air Station at Key West was buzzed by a saucer which was said to have been seen by hundreds of people. A destroyer escort had hastily put to sea to follow the course the machine had taken. (That was a hard one to swallow. The time it took for a destroyer to put to sea, the saucer, according

91

to the speed credited to it, would probably have been in Timbuctoo.) The same night Washington was visited by saucers again, and fighters sent up, of course, failed to intercept them.

Eight men, one of them a former Navy pilot, testified that they had seen a large metallic craft flying at an incredible speed at a high altitude over Manhattan Beach on July 27. They agreed that the unconventional aircraft had made no audible sound (not surprising at the altitude at which it was supposed to be flying), and it did not trail any visible exhaust. As it turned to the south it seemed to separate into seven round objects, three of them flying on in a V formation and the others following in pairs flying abreast. The pilot told the interrogating officer that it was as if a stack of coins had smoothly separated. After circling for a short while the group of U.F.O.s flew away. Could the men have witnessed a forerunner of a rocket with multiple warheads? Or were they thinking of "Pennies from Heaven"?

Newspapers now began playing a new tune. The public must be told without any more quibbling what the Government knew about U.F.O.s. One published explanation, put forward by American scientist Dr. Donald Menzel, was well known to scientists and had already been taken into account by U.S. Intelligence. This was the temperature inversion theory. Air normally grows colder as altitude increases, but under certain conditions there could be layers of warm air with cold layers beneath. The denser the medium, the slower light rays move through it, and they are refracted or bent as they pass from cold to warm air. That is how mirages in deserts occur, or what seem to motorists to be pools of water on the road ahead. Like light, radar waves also move more slowly in a dense medium and are refracted in the same way. Menzel's opinion was that what people had thought to be saucers were reflections of ground lights or of stars, the sun, or the moon, and what the scopes had shown as U.F.O.s had been deflected radar beams. Reflections of moving lights such as those on cars or trains gave the illusion of speed, acceleration, darting movements and manoeuvres. Motorists driving at night are well aware of the illusion of lights in the sky caused by lights reflected in their side windows. On August 3 at Hamilton Air Force Base, California, a formation of U.F.O.s seen hovering above the field by service personnel and picked up on Ground Control Intercept radar could well have been explained by Menzel's theory.

An unusual encounter with a Wellsian saucer was claimed by an American scoutmaster backed up by three young scouts. Driving home from a scout meeting on the night of August 19, 1952, they saw a mysterious, eerie light in the woods ahead. The scoutmaster left the boys in the car while he went ahead to scout armed with a machete (of all things) and a flashlight. One of the scouts who had remained in the car claimed that minutes later a sudden burst of flame had shafted down from just above the trees to the spot where the scoutmaster must be, and when he failed to return one boy made off to the nearest house and phoned the sheriff. The scoutmaster re-appeared from the wood just as the sheriff arrived on the scene. He said that he had reached a clearing in the wood when he sensed that something was hovering above him. He had flashed his light skyward and saw not far above the trees a metallic, disc-shaped craft about twenty-five feet in diameter. A turret in the machine had opened, and a jet of flame streaked from it, scorching his arm and burning his hat. The scoutmaster said he had been dazed and by the time he had recovered from the shock the saucer had gone. His arm was reddened and his hat was indeed scorched. But what did all that prove? It is not on record whether the scoutmaster swore on his scout's honour that the story was true.

This was not the first time that someone had claimed to have been burned by a flying saucer. Two boys in Amarillo, Texas, had reported that a small flying saucer had landed near them and they had approached it and saw that its top was spinning. One boy had touched the side of the craft, whereupon it had thrown off a hot gas or spray and had taken off immediately. The boy whose hand was, in fact, slightly scorched claimed that that was how it had happened, but not much credence was placed on the story.

On August 24 a jet pilot colonel en route to Turner Air Force Base in Georgia, flying a F-84 at 35,000 feet, reported having seen two round silver objects flying together over Hermanas, New Mexico. He said that they had flown around him for a short while and then suddenly accelerated and disappeared at a colossal speed. The colonel was debriefed by Intelligence and gave his story calmly and convincingly. It was probable that the U.F.O.s were top-secret experimental aircraft.

A musician working for a Kansas radio station was driving into Pittsburgh, Kansas, on the night of August 27. As dawn was breaking he saw something hovering above a field, and as he came closer he was able to make out a large contraption comprising two discs one above the other between which was a round cabin with three or four windows emitting a bluish light. The musician left his car, and as he approached the machine he thought he could see a shadowy figure through the window. Then there had come a low pulsating noise from within the machine and it had shot off straight up into the sky. There was no corroboration for this tale, but it was something to talk about.

At Sutton, West Virginia, thousands of people were said to have seen a saucer streak across the night sky, according to news reports on September 12. Not to be outdone, three young brothers and a seventeen-year-old youth thought they saw something strange on a hillside and went to investigate. The youth said he shone his flash-light on two shiny orbs and – horror of horrors! – there before them was a nine-foot monster with a red, sweaty face, eyes protruding on stalks a foot apart, and body glowing a dull green. Very monster-like, it emitted a hissing sound, whereupon the boys stopped to gaze no longer but fled. It was stated that the boys' faces were covered with an oily substance and that later that night they developed symptoms consistent with having been sprayed with mustard gas. The local sheriff and his men examined the area and found tracks on the ground, flattened grass, and fragments of some plastic-like material, but that was all. Perhaps the monster only seemed nine feet tall to the boys blundering on a farmer in protective clothing doing a spot of crop or tree spraying. If that was the case, the crop sprayer, whoever he was, kept his mouth shut for reasons of his own. Local astronomers said a meteor had passed over Sutton.

During September U.S. Air Force planes were scrambled several times to intercept U.F.O.s. On September 23, F-86s from March Air Force Base in California failed to identify a craft flying at over fifty thousand feet. On September 26, Air Force crews aboard planes approaching the Azores reported seeing strange green lights in the sky, but there had been so many apparently piffling reports of lights in the skies all over the world that service Intelligence investigators were themselves sparking blue lights whenever another saucer tale landed in their laps. There were hoaxes galore, and there seemed to be more people seeing saucers than there were seeing pink elephants, and that was a lot of people.

At Sale, near Manchester, on September 27, 1952, a woman claimed that while tending her garden she had seen a round bright silver object which was spinning like a top as it flew across the sky. A sighting was reported by two policeman in the Lake District, who said that the object was a golden ring like a moon skidding across Skiddaw Mountain in Cumberland. It was probably just moonshine.

Again there were reports of saucers from all over the world. They were variously described as being like dinner plates, bubbles, spheres, white balls of fire, torpedoes, or cigars. The manager of a photographic studio in Bulawayo, Rhodesia, produced a photograph which he claimed he had taken of a saucer flying over the city.

On September 29, a silver disc was sighted above N.A.T.O. naval vessels on exercises in the North Sea, apparently keeping the warships under surveillance. A photographer aboard the U.S. aircraft carrier *Franklin Roosevelt* was said to have taken three coloured pictures of the U.F.O. Two officers and three men of R.A.F. Coastal Command later reported that a Gloster Meteor jet taking part in the exercise had been followed back to base by a disc-shaped object. It was probably a Russian aircraft of a design not known to the Western powers at the time.

On the same day a large, shining metal disc with two smaller discs flying beneath it was seen over Karup Airfield and other parts of Denmark, and two days later a U.F.O. was seen near Bayonne, France. Five days after that the Press reported that many thousands of people in Denmark, northern Germany, and southern Sweden had seen U.F.O.s of the luminous and glowing variety.

From France came a story that on October 14 hundreds of people at Lens and Oléron had seen a cigar-shaped aircraft with an escort of shiny discs flying across the sky. Among those who had witnessed the startling apparitions were many leading citizens, including college professors at Oléron. Mont de Marsan Airfield confirmed that they had picked up a large image on their scope. A weird twist to the story was that one disc had discharged a flood of fine threads which had enveloped an eyewitness, holding him like a fly in a web. During World War II the British had often dropped showers of shredded tinfoil to jam German radar, and that might have been the inspiration for the story of the shower of fine threads. The man claiming to have been caught in a web was no doubt just trying an exercise in one-upmanship.

On December 4 a shaken Air Force pilot landed at Laredo, Texas, and reported that twelve miles from the field a blue-lighted U.F.O. had buzzed his F-51, missing him by inches. Furthermore it had circled the jet unbelievably fast and had then returned to make another pass at it. The pilot said he had switched off his lights and dived to one thousand feet. The saucer veered away, climbed, and disappeared.

Returning over the Gulf of Mexico to its base in Texas on December 6 after a night practice flight to Florida, a B-29 was about a hundred miles off the coast of Louisiana when the radar man picked up on his screen a U.F.O. that appeared to be approaching at somewhere in the region of five thousand miles per hour. A bluish light flashed by the B-29; then came more blips, and more saucers were seen heading for the bomber at a frightening speed. Still more blips, and another group of saucers flashed by. Smaller machines were seen to merge with a larger machine. Saucers? Or were they streaks of reflected lights converging from the coastline? The blips and spots on the radar? Dr. Menzel's theory had explained all that.

To see the year out, on December 29 there were reports of a U.F.O. sighting over northern Japan by the crews of three U.S. Air Force planes. This latest flying saucer had red, white, and green revolving lights. This sighting was confirmed by ground and airborne radar, and eleven days later a similar U.F.O. was again seen and tracked over Japan. It was probably a Russian Mig, a forerunner of the Foxbat that landed in Japan in August 1976.

At the start of 1953 the saucers were still going strong. One sighted over Dallas, Texas, at the beginning of January merely had blue and orange lights, unlike the Japanese sighting of January 9, which had sported red, green, and white lights. From Canton, Ohio, on January 11 came a report of two metallic discs seen by civilians, and from Kerryville, Texas, there were reports of a glowing red oval-shaped U.F.O.

By now everyone familiar with flying saucer stories knew of the glowing red-orange variety, the silvery metallic variety, the ball, the cigar, and the disc; but nobody ever claimed to have seen an object like a flying bedstead such as the contraptions that landed on the Moon or Mars. Laymen could not envisage anything but stream-lined objects streaking around in space, so they stuck to their stories of the stereotyped flying saucers.

In 1953 publicized sightings and radar trackings of U.F.O.s were mostly from U.S. Air Force personnel serving all over the world. From Rosalia (Washington), Truk (an island in the Pacific), Korea, Tunis, Tripoli, the Canal Zone, Britain, Australia, and South Africa, saucer sightings were reported.

According to a news item in the British Press in April 1953, three youths claimed to have seen a flying saucer over the outskirts of Sheffield and to have watched it for twenty-five minutes before it flew away. Nobody else claimed to have seen it.

On the night of May 2, 1953, a British Comet jet airliner took off from Dum Dum Airport, Calcutta, in driving rain. Six minutes later it disintegrated in mid-air, showering wreckage over an area of five square miles. Whatever had happened to the airliner had happened so suddenly that the pilot had had no time to signal the ground. Civil Air Ministry investigators concluded after an extensive examination of the wreckage that the Comet had been hit by an un-identified flying body. If it had there were no pieces of it among the wreckage. Had the plane been destroyed by a flying saucer? That was the question the newspapers liked to pose, although there was not the remotest evidence to suggest that the Comet had collided with any large body or had been hit by a missile. The question made good copy. Had the plane been struck by a meteorite or lightning? Very likely, but the saucer suggestion was more intriguing.

Any phenomenon the Press could even remotely connect with flying saucers was grist for the mill, whether there were logical explanations or not. On November 27, 1953, a double explosion and a shock-wave sweeping up the estuary of the Medway in Kent killed one man and injured another. From Shorne, near Gravesend, fifteen miles away, bright flashes had been seen in the noon sky, followed by the explosions. It could have been a naval shell bursting prematurely in the sky, an aircraft blowing up (though none was reported in the vicinity), or an experimental rocket exploding prematurely, but the question had to be posed: Was it a saucer?

More U.F.O. sightings were reported from other parts of England and Europe as well as America right until the end of 1953. They continued unabated through the next year, slackening off in 1955 except for an odd paragraph filler in a newspaper or two. Some sensational American pulp magazines still carried lurid saucer stories full of dire warnings of imminent peril to the world.

In 1956 there was a flying saucer scare at Preston, Lancashire, where hundreds of people phoned the police and the newspapers to say that they had seen a round silvery object spinning in the sky. A plane was sent up to investigate and the pilot said the mystery object appeared to be a meteorological balloon. But that was too simple an answer. According to the Press no such balloon was unaccounted

1950s pin-up: more akin to
naturism than eroticism.

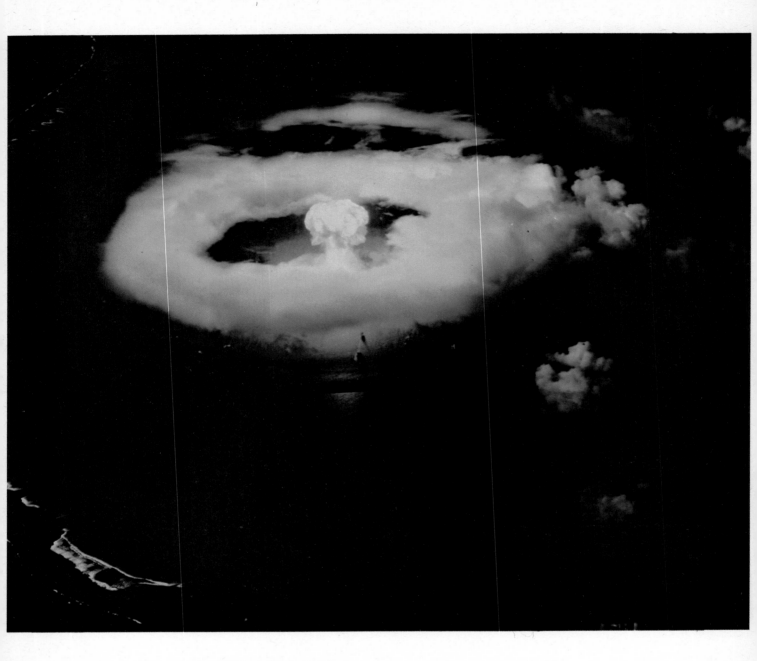

Bikini Atoll: the A-bomb
explosion is forgotten, the
two-piece swimsuit never.

POPPERPHOTO

for. It surely was a balloon, however. Large plastic balloons carrying pamphlets in a foreign language were later reported to have landed at various places near London that day and one had exploded. The balloons and pamphlets had been confiscated by the police, which was hardly surprising. The Western powers were distributing propaganda pamphlets over Eastern Europe during this period, by balloons which were timed to explode in mid-air and scatter the leaflets far and wide. The balloons seen over various parts of England, which, of course, had to be called flying saucers, were probably some of the propaganda bombs gone astray. In December, a young man claimed he had taken a pot shot at a saucer hovering over his garden and had scored a hit.

Apparently 1957 was a very good year for saucers over England, with U.F.O.s being reported all over the country from Oban to the Channel. There were green balls, red balls, and whitish-yellow balls. They were fiery, glowing, and pulsating. There were round ones, cigar ones, and discs, and so on and on, right to the end of the decade. In America, even in the sixties, newspapers and magazines were still making capital out of saucer revivals, serving American radio and television with publicity for a host of space series such as "The Aliens" and "U.F.O.". The Press still made the old claim that there was a conspiracy at the Pentagon to hush up U.F.O. stories, but it was all old hat and they failed to make people's flesh creep.

Nobody has so far topped the saucer story of George Adamski, who operated a refreshment stand on the road leading to Palomar Observatory in California. Describing himself as a former professor of that establishment, Adamski, who had produced a number of pictures purporting to be of flying saucers, recounted a remarkable story to a newspaper writer with his eye on the main chance.

Adamski and some friends had gone into the desert "to keep watch for a space ship", and after a while he had gone off alone to a spot a bit further afield to keep a lone vigil. Sure enough, the redoubtable Adamski was rewarded for his patience when to his astonishment a round machine some twenty feet in diameter landed near him. Adamski signalled to his friends to join him, and they all saw a man from space climb out of the machine and look about him. He was about twenty-three years old and had a tanned, weather-beaten face, greyish-green eyes, and long sandy hair which flowed below his collar. He was wearing a brown Eisenhower jacket, ski pants, and reddish-brown shoes. He spoke a little English and a language which sounded like Chinese but was possibly Serbo-Croat, or even Russian. He indicated by signs that he had come from another ship hovering five hundred miles above the earth.

When the man from space had finally sailed away to join his companions, Adamski saw that the soles of the spaceman's shoes had made strange impressions on the ground that looked like hiero-glyphics. Now, as luck would have it, one of Adamski's friends happened to have some plaster of Paris in his pocket (something no spaceship-watcher should be without), and casts were made of the spaceman's left-footed message. Unfortunately no translation of the message has ever been made, and if Adamski knew what it was all about he was not telling. But a beatnik from outer space wearing an Eisenhower jacket! Nobody else had thought of that.

At the moment flying saucer headlines are out of fashion. More recently it has been the turn of the Loch Ness monster to hog media space. However, like cowboys and Indians, flying saucers will no doubt go the full circle and be back, perhaps next time with psyche-delic lights.

The cowboy was king

WHEN I WAS YOUNG MY SCREEN HEROES WERE, NATURALLY enough, cowboys. Tom Mix, Hoot Gibson, Jack Hoxie, and Buck Jones were my favourites, and like most kids I rode the backyard range mounted on my favourite broomstick, Tony, and lassoed cats with the clothes-line. There were no toy cowboy suits for us in those days. My outfit consisted of an old punched-up trilby hat of my father's with the brim turned down all round, which dropped down well over my ears, a none too clean handkerchief tied round my neck, my braces tied round my waist, and a toy pistol stuck in them. No doubt I looked about as much like a cowboy as the Artful Dodger. I suppose I had hopes that one day I would actually meet some cowboy film stars in the flesh, and that was about all.

By the time I came out of the Army I had long since lost interest in cowboys and Indians, although I had seen a fair share of Western films while serving in the Forces. But when, after writing a series of cheap, but highly successful, private detective stories, I was asked to try my hand at a few Westerns I had to revive my interest and brush up on Western terminology and backgrounds to give some authenticity to my tales. I had read Zane Grey and vaguely recalled *Riders of the Purple Sage*, *West of Pecos*, *The Thundering Herd*, and *Code of the West*, and of course I was familiar with Clarence E. Mumford's "Bar 20" novels and his original *Hopalong Cassidy*. On occasion I had dipped into Smith and Street Western pulp magazines.

I did not keep any of the Westerns I wrote (to tell the truth, I never keep anything), but I do recall that *Apache Arroyo* was one of the titles. I did not like writing Westerns and only did it for the money, which was very little, to be sure. At a later date I did produce Western pulp magazines and paperbacks for another publisher, but then I was not required to write the stories.

At all events, I found myself heavily involved with Westerns and cowboy characters from the beginning of the fifties right up to the end of the decade. It all started when I had a studio in Gower Street, London, and was producing comic strips and comic books for several publishers. A very keen and energetic young friend of mine, Douglas Endersby, whom I had met whilst producing a comic called *The*

Roy Rogers with the author
and Douglas Endersby.

Sheriff for his publisher, had somehow managed to establish himself
in my office, from which he started promoting publicity in Britain
for the great American cowboy singing star Roy Rogers.

Douglas set up the "Roy Rogers Fan Club", and produced the
Roy Rogers Review, a monthly fan magazine. His constant dashing about
and long phone calls, which not only cramped my style but which
I also paid for, were bad enough, but he contrived to enlist my
aid in every possible way. He would ask me to do "just a small
line drawing, it won't take a tick", or to write "just a few words
of copy", or to do "just a small layout", for which I would be
paid "in due course". (Twenty-five years is a long wait for "due
course", as I mentioned to him on the phone only the other day,
to which he replied, "Don't break your heart. I'll give you a ride
in my Rolls." He was sincere. He always was.)

Actually we had a good deal of fun with the Roy Rogers promotion
for which I was roped in. The highlight was in 1952 when we organized

100

a national competition with *T.V. Comic* in conjunction with the *News of the World*, which then owned it. The big prize for the winner was a trip to New York to meet Roy Rogers himself at his rodeo show in Madison Square Garden. The editor of *T.V. Comic* was "Bloss" Lewis, a one-time *News of the World* cartoonist, and he told us that there were over eighty thousand entries for the competition. The editorial department had decided that the winner of the competition had to be a boy, had to be typically robust and British, confident and articulate, as he would be appearing on American TV and radio.

After a number of interviews in various parts of the country, a boy from the South Coast was finally chosen as the winner and brought by his mother to a London hotel, where Douglas and I first met him. He was robust all right, and it soon became obvious that he was going to prove more than a handful for Douglas, who was to accompany him to New York. In fact, no sooner had his mother departed, leaving the lad in Douglas' charge, than Douglas clipped his ear and told him that was just for starters and there would be more clips all the way from the Regent Palace Hotel to New York and back if he did not simmer down. But the boy was not in the least intimidated. I wished Douglas the best of British and left him to it. As it turned out the lad played his part well in America except that he happened to be a bed-wetter, and Douglas said that he soon had to give up clouting him as it was not the lad's ear that was getting thick but his own hand.

Not long after the competition promotion, Roy Rogers came to England, and Douglas and I went to his reception at the Savoy Hotel. Present were Roy's large retinue, British licensees of Roy Rogers products, the Press, promoters, and a lot of other funny people. Roy was cheerful, charming, and quiet-spoken. The others were not cheerful, not charming, and spoke loudly.

Roy was the first screen cowboy I had ever met (although I had met a number of Americans during the war who claimed to be cowboys), and he was nothing like I had imagined a cowboy to be. He looked city-bred. His clothes, which were well tailored and immaculate but too stylized and artificial, his cowboy boots, which were too fancy, and his hat, which he never removed, would probably have set back any normal working cowboy a month's pay. I do not remember if I had expected to see him in Levi's, a plaid woollen shirt, and neckerchief, but to me he looked more like an amiable Texan oil baron than a cowboy. Roy laughed when I mentioned this to him, and said he was sure that had he appeared at the Savoy in Levi's he would have been thrown out. He was probably right. He assured me that as a youngster he had thought that the clothes of his own cowboy heroes were a little too fancy but now he had to play the game.

Another cowboy I met many times was Norman Harper from Canada, who toured Britain in the fifties. I was drawing a strip cartoon for *Wonderman* comics featuring Norman and his horse Starlight, and

Lloyd Goffe, Norman Harper, and his horse Starlight in the Temple.

I arranged a publicity stunt for him and a West Ham speedway rider, Lloyd Goffe, known to his fans as "Cowboy" Goffe. We arranged to meet in the Inner Temple, where John Alexander, at that time photographer for the *Speedway Gazette*, would do his stuff.

On a quiet Sunday morning, Norman and his manager drove into the square trailing a horse-box. Norman brought out his horse and mounted up just as Goffe appeared on his motorbike. Alexander took pictures of them mounted on each others steeds, with changes of hats, and my young son wearing an Eskimo outfit trying to get into the act. (It was a cold day in winter.)

Then the Press turned up, and so did a policeman who told us that sort of thing was not allowed in the Inner Temple and in fact no vehicles should park without permission. However, the upshot was photographs of the policeman in a cowboy's hat and a cowboy in a policeman's hat. My son had great fun. The next day there was a good picture in an evening newspaper captioned "Cowboy in the Inner Temple".

A few years later I was commissioned to produce covers for American comic books which included many that featured cowboy film stars. Soon I was drawing coloured covers for *Tom Mix*, *Ken Maynard*, *Lash Larue*, *Rod Cameron*, *Tex Ritter*, *Hopalong Cassidy*, *Bob Steele*, *Rocky Lane*, *Monte Hale*, and many others. I also produced pages for the comic books.

As I was already involved in producing his comic books, when Tex Ritter came to Britain in 1952 I was saddled with the job of promoting him and his products and doling out the licences. There were ties, badges, suits, guns, holsters, painting books, and annuals, and soon my son had a cowboy suit for every day of the week and a set of pistols to go with each one.

I used to meet Tex early every morning in his hotel suite to discuss business matters and invariably found him still in bed. He would be sitting up reading a newspaper, eating his breakfast from a tray, and wearing his stetson. He would swing out of bed, put on his cowboy boots, then, as naked as a jay bird except for hat and boots, go into the bathroom. Tex was one of the most pleasant and likeable men I have ever met. He was a first-class country and western singer, and during our morning bull sessions he used to run up and down the scales and sing snatches of songs. He was always merry and bright, and the Irish chambermaid idolized him.

On several occasions I went to see him at Harringay Arena, where he was appearing in a Western spectacular, and one day I went with him from his dressing room to meet his horse wrangler in the arena, where dozens of horses were being exercised before the show. The air was vibrant and steamy and the smell was enough to knock anyone back ten feet.

"Phew!" I spluttered, "what a pen and ink!"

The author and Tex Ritter shake on a deal.

103

Tex Ritter signs a contract
for the author.

"Huh?" said Tex.

"Huh?" said the horse wrangler.

"The stink," I said, "how can anyone stand it?"

Tex grinned, sniffed appreciatively, and said, "Stink? What stink? I can't smell anything." And the horse wrangler shook his head. Even if they were used to the smell, I still think they were putting me on.

The show at Harringay Arena was billed as Tom Arnold's Western Spectacle "Texas" – and spectacle it certainly was. Presented by the impresarios Tom Arnold and Francis S. Gentle, devised and produced by Clem Butson, the show comprised twenty events which included trick riding, roping, knife throwing, and bronc riding, as well as cowboy singing and music and Indian tribal dances by Asah Indians.

The announcer, Cal McCord, whom I had met several times, was a Canadian cowboy who had acquired a host of fans through his tremendous popularity in the B.B.C. series "Riders of the Range".

Also in the show was an old favourite with British audiences, Tex McLeod, a Texan who had been a friend of Will Rogers and who had become a champion rodeo star before entering the wider field of show business by appearing in the Ziegfeld Follies in New York. He had been brought to London by the great impresario C. B. Cochran to feature in a London revue and stayed to tour the halls with his lasso and rope spinning act.

Another rodeo star was Buff Brady, billed as a world champion trick rider and roper, who included in his act turning a complete somersault in the saddle "simultaneously lassooing a passing galloping steed; standing on his head on horseback roping and pulling in galloping horses and then his most spectacular feat, roping and catching five horses in one throw." Cowgirls in the show included trick and fancy riders Pat Paul and Texas Rodeo Queen Jenny Portwood, both from the Lone Star State.

The troupe of Asah Indians of rodeo and Hollywood fame performed a fine selection of dances from the Eagle, Gourd, Shield, Hoop, Snake, and Pipe series, and slow and fast war dances. Television and rodeo star Karen Greer, wearing striking Cherokee costume and seated on a beautiful Apaloosa mare, sang songs which included "The Virgin Sun" and "Moon Festival" in her remarkable voice that ranged through four octaves.

The star of the show, Tex Ritter, rode slowly into the arena mounted on his horse White Flash and sang his numbers without dismounting. Unbeknown to the audience he had to be helped into the saddle as he was suffering from hernia trouble, and this he found amusing. Tex, who had originally studied law at the University of Texas, starred in many Western films, was on television regularly, and was a popular recording star with R.C.A. His records included "Deck of Cards", "Rye Whiskey", "Daddy's Last Letter", "Home on the Range", "Old Chisholm Trail", and "There's a Moon over My Shoulder". He later achieved even greater fame as a country and western singer, and his record of the famous theme song "Do Not Foresake Me, Oh My Darling", from the soundtrack of the movie *High Noon*, was top of the hit parade.

During the fifties I must have produced at least a dozen regular Western comic books as well as Western pulp magazines and annuals. Except for British versions of Spanish Westerns, the last I saw of the old Western strips was about ten years ago when I ran the Lone Ranger as a regular strip feature in *T.V. Tornado*, the weekly comic I was producing.

Hi-yo, Silver! Away!

It was said in 1952 that if youngsters had had the vote, Roy Rogers could easily have run for President. And why not? – Ronald Reagan chanced his arm with far fewer fans. Roy Rogers was born Leonard Slye in Cincinatti, Ohio, in 1912. A former farm boy, he was popular with children and also with thousands of adults, judging by the crowds that turned out to greet him in cities, towns, and villages when he was on tour, and by the countless masses who followed his shows on TV and radio, and in the cinema.

Millions of dollars were spent by Roy's doting public on cowboy gear, comic books, games, puzzles, and anything else promoted by the King of the Cowboys. Roy was big business. Not only did his personal tours and shows all over the United States bounce up the cash registers; they also promoted the sale of his goods, so all in all he was a veritable money-making machine.

In one typical month Roy performed in the Madison Square Garden Rodeo, saw the release on Broadway of the film *Son of Paleface*, in which he co-starred with Bob Hope and Jane Russell, and launched his own weekly television show, on N.B.C. in the much-coveted 6.30 to 7 p.m. slot on Sundays. Always Roy made headlines wherever he went. The publicity hounds were busy all the time dreaming up ideas to smooth the way for Roy and his famous white horse, Trigger.

Yet Roy was always an amiable, easy-to-meet, lovable guy, and this endeared him to youngsters throughout the world as well as to adults who recognized him as a good influence. He lived with his wife, Dale Evans, who co-starred with him in many of his movies, and their family of four children, Cheryl, Linda Lou, Dusty, and Robin, on a sprawling five-acre ranch in Encino which, except for the usual Hollywood-style swimming pool fenced for safety with a removable wire fence, was more like a typical Ohio spread. The ranch-house was packed with sporting gear, hunting trophies and prizes, and heavy furniture. When his old friend Trigger died, Roy had him stuffed and mounted just like one of his trophies.

On Highland Avenue in downtown Hollywood a rambling modern office building housed the headquarters of the mighty Roy Rogers Enterprises, presided over by Roy's personal manager and friend from way back in the Ohio days, Art Rush. Between films, TV and radio programmes, recordings, and personal appearances, and the all too brief periods at home with the wife and children, Roy contrived to spend a little time conferring with his business staff, but understandably most of the time his own imposing office was empty.

The move into the big time started one day in 1938 when a wide-shouldered, lean-hipped lad, with the high cheekbones of an Indian brave and the vivid blue eyes of a Viking, appeared before a motion picture camera for the first time. He plucked a chord or two on his well-worn guitar, sang "Listen to the Rhythm of the Range" for Republic Pictures, and plunged up to his neck in Western movies and dollars.

Until that day Roy had been just one of the hundreds of almost unknown balladeers appearing at barn dances or on the radio with Western groups. After leaving the farm in Ohio, Roy had worked his way through New Mexico as a cowhand before drifting to

California. In order to make a living between infrequent singing engagements, he worked with state road gangs and even picked fruit. He was always popular with his workmates and entertained them with his singing and guitar playing. In 1937 he sang on the radio in "Under Western Stars" and "The Old Barn Dance", and then in 1938 he got the break that would make him one of the most popular stars of the film industry's entire history, with a far-ranging appeal that boosted him into a one-man multi-million-dollar business proposition. *Son of Paleface*, a two-million-dollar Technicolor production made by Paramount in 1952, was Roy's eighty-ninth movie.

The Madison Square World Championship Rodeo starred Roy Rogers at the highest guarantee and percentage figure ever offered at that venue. Immediately before this, in January and February 1952, Roy had appeared at the annual Houston Fatstock Show and Rodeo, where he stacked up the biggest attendance record and the biggest gross profits in the show's twenty-year history, with every performance a complete sell-out.

His TV show on N.B.C., "The Roy Rogers Show", was sponsored by the Post Cereals Division of General Foods. Under a three-year contract with Post Cereals and a seven-year one with N.B.C., Roy himself produced the specially filmed half-hour Westerns with all rights reverting to him after the first two showings. A taped series for the same sponsor and the same network was "The Roy Rogers Show" on radio.

In record shops all over the United States, Canada, and Britain, "California Rose" backed by "Four-legged Friend", two songs Roy sang in *Son of Paleface*, sold in their thousands. The record was the fifty-sixth Roy had made, most of them under the RCA-Victor label. Department stores and toy-shops all over the world sold merchandise bearing the Roy Rogers trade mark from dozens of licensees of Roy Rogers Enterprises working on a royalty basis. In 1951, for example, 21,000,000 dollars' worth of merchandise was sold, and that represented wholesale terms only. Sears Roebuck, the American mail order company, alone accounted for 7,500,000 dollars of it.

How was it that a poor farm lad who had had to leave high school early to earn a living in the years of the Great Depression managed to reach a position where for year after year he was the top earner for the film company for which he worked and for his own enterprises? First of all, he had the looks, the intrinsic appeal, and the personality to distinguish him from the hundreds of other cowboy singers going the rounds at that time. His were qualities that drama schools and charm schools still cannot manufacture, no matter how well they can smooth rough spots and teach techniques and method. Another quality that stood Roy in good stead was his dedication and the fact that he had been "movie struck" from an early age and had persevered in his efforts to emulate his cowboy heroes Tom Mix, Buck Jones, and Hoot Gibson. But not in his wildest dreams did he ever think that one day he would find himself in the cowboy hall of fame.

Even when he arrived in California and joined such groups as the Sons of the Pioneers Roy did not foresee the heights to which he would rise. Infrequent paid engagements meant he had to supplement his income by taking construction labouring jobs, and any other jobs, for that matter, to keep on eating, and Roy had a healthy appetite. But still Roy kept plugging away at what he considered to be his professional career, always hoping and always on the lookout for an opportunity to show what he could really do.

One day, by chance, while he was in a music store much frequented by cowboy singers, Roy overheard some of them talking and one mentioned that Republic Pictures were auditioning cowboy singers and that it might be worthwhile "putting on the dog and moseying along". That was enough for Roy. He went out of that store like a streak and galloped off to the film studios.

From that day forth Roy never looked back. In his first year with Republic he made four pictures, and in the second year, as a fully fledged star, another nine. When, in 1938, Roy acquired the palomino horse Trigger, a partnership was formed that would capture the hearts and the imaginations of youngsters all over the world.

Art Rush was among the first to realize the enormous potential of the new cowboy star in commercial fields other than filming. He was quick to see that Roy took advantage of any possibility to "turn a buck or two", and besides arranging recordings, rodeos, and personal appearances for his cowboy star client Art also set up deals with publishing companies, including the British company World Distributors (Manchester) Ltd., to produce *The Roy Rogers Comic Book* and annuals, the sales of which reached over twenty-five million in the early fifties. In addition, Art leased the Rogers name to Sackville Brothers for the manufacture and sale on a royalty basis of cowboy playsuits and hats.

When Gene Autry, hitherto Republic's number one cowboy singing star, moved over to Columbia, it was inevitable that Roy should succeed to the title. Roy's films were rolling out of the studio thick and fast, each more popular than the last, and such films as *Red River Valley*, *Man from Cheyenne*, and *South of Santa Fé* brought in fat profits for the studio. Soon in the Motion Picture-Fame Magazine's annual poll of more than thirteen thousand film exhibitors Roy was dubbed King of the Cowboys – and there was nobody to dispute it.

When he first acquired Trigger, Roy was only an average rider and far from being a spectacular performer, but before long he and his horse had developed a sort of empathy with each other and Roy's riding began to show the touch of class that gave the hallmark stamp to his cowboy image. In the rodeo arena Roy showed his ability with horses by his handling of eight palominos in a sensational act that brought the crowds roaring to their feet. His horse wrangler

Marvelman: nostalgia for
Nasty Tales's readers?

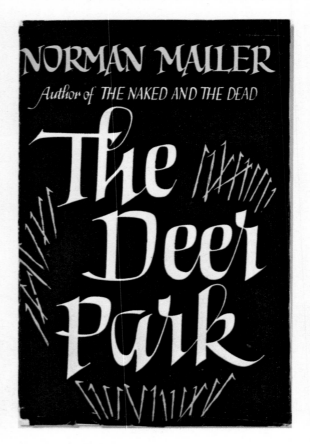

Novels of the 1950s: still
being read?

Gene Autry, the singing cowboy of the forties, who was succeeded by Roy Rogers.

Our current production plans call for six pictures a year for Columbia release. In fulfilling that commitment, we want to thank exhibitors everywhere for their solid approval of this program which provides a NEW Autry picture of top quality EVERY TWO MONTHS.

GENE AUTRY Productions

Executive Producer ARMAND SCHAEFER

Already in Release

GENE AUTRY and CHAMPION "THE STRAWBERRY ROAN"
In Cinecolor · Directed by John English

GENE AUTRY and CHAMPION "THE LAST ROUNDUP"
Directed by John English

GENE AUTRY · BARBARA BRITTON "LOADED PISTOLS"
with CHAMPION · Directed by John English

GENE AUTRY and CHAMPION "THE BIG SOMBRERO"
In Cinecolor · Directed by Frank McDonald

GENE AUTRY and CHAMPION "RIDERS OF THE WHISTLING PINES"
Directed by John English

GENE AUTRY and CHAMPION "RIM OF THE CANYON"
Directed by John English

To Be Released

GENE AUTRY and CHAMPION "THE COWBOY AND THE INDIANS"
Directed by John English

GENE AUTRY and CHAMPION "SONS OF NEW MEXICO"

GENE AUTRY and CHAMPION "BARBED WIRE" (Tentative Title)
Directed by John English

GENE AUTRY and CHAMPION "BEYOND THE PURPLE HILLS"

kept Roy's large string of horses, which included a reserve for Trigger, like a first-class stable of racehorses. On tour, Trigger travelled in a specially designed, super de luxe air-conditioned horse trailer, chrome trimmed and leather lined, that had cost a small fortune. The wisdom of the infinite care and feeding of the horses was shown in the phenomenal success of Roy's rodeo appearances in New York, Detroit, and Houston.

Like most film studios, Republic Pictures regarded radio broadcasts by their stars as valuable publicity for the studio's pictures, and for three years Roy starred in his own weekly radio show on Mutual Broadcasting System's 567 stations. But it was a different kettle of fish when it came to television, for the film company feared that Roy on the box might keep customers away from the cinema. In 1951 Roy fell out with Republic Pictures over the question of television shows and he sought the termination of his contract with them. The studios maintained that film contracts forbade their stars to appear in television roles. Roy, for his part, contended that his film contract, containing no agreement on the signing of commercial endorsements, forbade the film company to release any films made by him to television for showing under commercial sponsorship or accompanied by advertising. The court upheld this viewpoint, and an injunction was slapped on Republic Pictures preventing them from releasing any of Roy's films to television companies. Roy was then free to go ahead and make films especially for television without finding himself in competition with the films he had made for Republic. He signed contracts with N.B.C. and Post Cereals for both television and radio, the first show appearing in 1951.

Each of the new half-hour Western films Roy made especially for television was complete in itself and had to be meticulously planned to fit in with his busy schedule, and Roy assembled an experienced team of film technicians to produce his pictures. Only a few months after the first Roy Rogers film on television, the show won *T.V. Digest*'s audience popularity poll as the number one Western show.

Roy Rogers fan clubs abounded. The Roy Rogers Riders Club organized by Al Rackin boasted two million members and operated in over two thousand American cinemas. The club show would open with a special feature film made by Roy which started with his "Cowboy Prayer", during which, it was reported, the youngsters would sit with bowed heads. Perhaps some did.

Unlike most other places in Encino Roy's ranch boasted no palm trees. He preferred to maintain the Ohio appearance of his home. Outhouses included quarters for his dogs, of which he kept quite a few – sometimes as many as thirty including hunting hounds. One of the outhouses contained a huge deep-freeze to stock the fish and game that Roy had brought home from his hunting trips.

Of course, the King of the Cowboys was no longer the Roy who had worked making roads, nor the Roy who had picked fruit for

a living, nor even Roy the cowboy balladeer. Fame and fortune had given him confidence, authority, independence, and the opportunity to do pretty much everything he desired. He certainly enjoyed the material advantages success had brought him, but he never hankered after the high life, which had never interested him even in the days when he was still struggling to make his way. Night clubs, hard drinking, big parties to celebrate nothing, and smart chit chat had not appealed to him then and did not appeal to him now.

Some people who are thankful for their good fortune in life find religion. Roy and Dale became active members of the Fountain Avenue Baptist Church in Hollywood, and when they were asked by evangelist Billy Graham to come to one of his gatherings in

Roy Rogers rides in triumph in Houston, Texas, in 1952.

Houston, Texas, they flew out from Hollywood late on a Saturday evening even though it meant a gruelling weekend as they had to be back on the movie set at seven on Monday morning.

It had been widely rumoured that when he spoke to that vast congregation in Houston, Roy would renounce his career in order to become a preacher. But that was never Roy's intention. From the pulpit he announced that he did not intend to give up his career and that he thought he could reach more people astride Trigger than by preaching publicly. He felt sure that as a cowboy he had more influence with youngsters to keep them on the right path.

The age of Marvelman

AT THE BEGINNING OF THE FIFTIES I HAD A STUDIO IN GOWER Street, Euston, consisting of four rooms with low, subsiding plaster ceilings on the top floor of a tatty Victorian terrace building. It had originally been a none too salubrious flat and, as one artist remarked on the day I moved in, it had all the makings of a first-class studio for starving artists. It was garret-like, had plenty of scope for untidiness, and was almost impregnable to unwelcome callers. The studio could only be reached by a long climb up four or five flights of rickety stairs with a two-inch-deep sink and cold water tap on the last landing before one reached the curtained glass-windowed door. The weary clump of footsteps and the creaking staircase would put one on the alert, and a quick glance through the curtains would tell if the visitor was to be tolerated or not.

It was in the Gower Street Studios that a good many of the completely independent comic books, periodicals, and magazines of the fifties were produced. The first of a long string of comic titles was for the Arnold Book Company run by Arnold Miller, ex-R.A.F., physically tough, shrewd, scrupulously fair and honest in his dealings. He favoured space strips at the time, and our first title was *Captain Valiant*, which was designed to lend itself to the merchandizing of gimmicks. So we drew our hero complete with uniform, weapons, and accessories to attract the attention of toy-makers, and they did.

Captain Vic Valiant of the Interplanetary Police Patrol wore a sort of blue boiler suit with the I.P.P. device on one breast pocket, a helmet sprouting a miniature television aerial, a cross belt with several self-propelled high explosive grenades, an anti-gravity belt round his waist, a space pistol, and, for good measure, an easy-to-manufacture round anti-blast shield bearing the I.P.P. device. One manufacturer marketed suit, helmet, goggles, and shield; another, space gun, grenades, whistles, and various other bits and pieces such as medals, badges, and insignia. My young son was very proud of his Captain Valiant outfit manufactured by Playtogs.

Besides the Captain Valiant comic, a Captain Valiant strip appeared regularly in the *ABC Film Review*. Fans applied to join the I.P.P.

and received badges and membership cards. After a while I drew only the cover and wrote brief story-lines and instructions for the artists. Roy Parker, an ex-soldier who had served with PAIFORCE during the war, drew a number of strips for Captain Valiant, but it was Colin Page who drew most of the subsequent pages. Especially successful was Colin's Insecto series in which the I.P.P. were involved in a war against intelligent giant locust-like beings from another planet. Colin rode a motorbike and always arrived dressed in helmet and leathers like a speedway rider, carrying his drawings rolled in a metal tube slung across his back.

Roy was working on our new comic for the Arnold Book Company, *Space Commando*. This was about the adventures of Space Commodore Sparky Malone and a special commando group equipped to operate in deep space. The drawings, of necessity quickly executed, were nevertheless effective, and there was nothing crude about the depictions of all kinds of spacecraft featured in the stories.

Another space comic in the same vein followed *Space Commando*. This was *Space Commander Kerry*, featuring the adventures of Space Commander Steve Kerry, fearless leader of the Interplanetary Special Service, and his two lieutenants, Rick Shaw and Tubby. Kerry's boys were equipped with a variety of suits and weapons, including a Volta handgun I.S.S. pattern, operating on deadly-pressure flash or temporary-paralysis ray; a contra-gravity auto flying belt used when within gravitational range of planets; and a rocket propulsion unit for use in outer space. Also featured in the comic was a strip called "Space Pilot" about Squadron Leader Rafe Marlow, space ace of the United Planets Forces and leader of Demon Squadron of the spacecraft carrier *Trident*.

At about this time, Bob Monkhouse, whom I knew as a talented comic-strip artist, had started writing a radio show entitled "Calling All Forces" starring Tony Hancock, Jimmy Edwards, and Petula Clark. Not having an office in town, he decided to move in on me with his partner, Denis Goodwin. A young friend of mine starting up as a publicity agent, also without an office, got wind of this and promptly moved in too. We were cramped and at times I was upset a good deal more than somewhat, but we managed to live with each other despite numerous clashes of temperament. I did not mind the company, but I did resent not being able to use my phone, which was often, especially as I was usually left to pay the bills. Gower Street Studios was a madhouse, but work poured out of there.

Ace Malloy was our fourth comic and was about air warfare in the jet age. Our heroes were mostly pilots flying Sabre jets in Korea in combat with red-starred Mig fighters. One of the artists for this comic had been a jet pilot and his artwork had the authentic touch. I drew the cover and a set of strips, but by now all of us were working under great pressure having to draw anything from ten to twelve pages of strips every week, and there was little time for finesse. Arnold said that what impressed the kids most in comics was

The great but tragic comedian Tony Hancock.

spontaneity, action, and punchy dialogue; they were not looking for Rembrandt and Shakespeare.

Independent comics were produced on a slim budget and artists had to maintain a high output in order to earn a living. In order to compete with big publishing houses the independent publisher had to cut his costs to the bone. His distribution was hampered through discrimination, not being able to afford to advertise, and the ever-rising costs of paper and printing. His individual print runs were

115

small, yet his titles rolled regularly off the presses, and without promotion and advertising his overall sales were in the region of a million comics per month.

Unlike big publishers the independent publisher had little fat in his organization. He made package deals in which he was supplied with all he needed for a flat fee. We who supplied the package had no fat at all in our loose-knit organization. We had no editors who were frustrated artists and writers, with assistants, secretaries, and typists; nobody who had to justify their existence by nit-picking, chipping in with their two-penn'orth and attending endless editorial meetings. Indeed, we had no editorial meetings as such, just an occasional bull session, and everything was informal. Our artwork, lettering, and printing were not the best by academic standards, but the stories were good, and taking into account the time factor, pressures, and costs, the comics were masterpieces and did their job more than adequately. The proof of the pudding was in the eating. We always had bags of mail from satisfied customers, the kids and the parents, and our publishers made money.

My assistant was a Canadian girl, Margaret Paton. An excellent artist, she often inked in my pencil drawings and made colour overlays for covers. Besides the covers we produced for the Arnold Book Company, we also produced covers for L. Miller and Son, and among the regular monthly titles were the Captain Marvel series; *Monte Hale, Bill Boyd, Hopalong Cassidy, Tex Ritter, Rocky Lane, Lash Larue, Tom Mix, Bob Steele, Rod Cameron, Ken Maynard*, and *Six Gun Heroes*, all Westerns; *Popeye, Captain Midnight, Spymaster*; as well as sundry Romance titles. We also produced regular filler pages and strips for a number of these titles.

Among Len Miller's most successful series were the Captain Marvel titles, reprints of Fawcett's of New York: *Captain Marvel, Captain Marvel Jr., The Marvel Family*, and *Mary Marvel*. One day Len phoned and said he wanted to see me urgently. Fawcett's were involved in some legal trouble with *Superman* over *Captain Marvel*; an injunction had been slapped on them, and Len said it looked as if his supply of American material for *Captain Marvel* would be cut off. Had I any ideas? I had, and for my trouble received a regular supply of work for the next six years.

In the last of the Marvel titles we announced that Captain Marvel and Captain Marvel Jr. were so well known as marvelmen that in future they would be known by the titles Marvelman and Young Marvelman and would each have a weekly comic of their own, and the Marvel Family would henceforth appear as the Marvelman Family in a monthly comic. There was no hitch, no hiatus. The new titles were greeted with increased sales, and letters poured in from enthusiastic kids demanding a "Marvelman Club". I was not too pleased about that as I wanted no part in the time-consuming job of running a club. Luckily for me, however, that problem was dealt with at the publishing house.

Marvelman – from a comic
of the fifties.

Preparing the transition from Marvel to Marvelman had its problems but was not too difficult. We never used elaborate blow-by-blow scripts for our artists. I credited artists with imagination and did not want to tie them rigidly to tight scripts. Often writers with little conception of an artist's problems would blithely call for a frame, say four inches wide by three inches deep, depicting a crowd scene with a man on the right laughing while reading a book entitled *A Day at the Races with the Right People*; four men in the centre of the scene playing cards, all hands to be shown; two men fighting; and another man handing his son a 1947 threepenny piece to go buy an ice-cream.

For a time one of my brothers, Andy, wrote a one- or two-page story-line and the artist interpreted it the way he saw it and in as many frames as he saw fit. I drew a standard depiction for all the main characters, including the villainous Gargunza created by my brother. The artists based their characters on my drawings, but each with his own individual stamp. However, any arbitrary deviation from the salient points of the characterization, dress, and capabilities of Marvelman laid down in the original specifications was not tolerated.

Don Lawrence, the first of the Marvelman artists, drew Marvelman with long legs and slender ankles, and all his characters were elongated. Roy Parker's character had bulging muscles and a lantern jaw. John Whitlock had his Marvelman stockily built with a barrel chest, as did Norman Light. Light's characters always appeared to be slightly asymetrical, what we used to call "one up and one down eyed".

Roy's backgrounds were stylized, but were detailed, precise, and interesting, with multi-windowed skyscrapers, accurately girdered bridges, and his vehicles, mechanical devices, weapons, and spaceships were authentic-looking. Roy's drawing was always clean black and white with a minimum of cross-hatching. Don's drawings were looser, and his character delineations usually more interesting. He was not long out of art school and Marvelman was his first commission.

Self-taught artist John Whitlock was a busy charter pilot whose passion was drawing comic strips. He often used to sketch while his plane was on automatic pilot, and I once received a large packet of Marvelman drawings posted to me from Singapore where a charter flight had taken him. His style was reminiscent of the American artist Milton Caniff, and he often introduced boldly drawn authentic aircraft into his stories.

Another regular Marvelman artist was curly-haired Frank Daniels, who looked more like a bespectacled young business executive than a black and white artist. His style was spidery, sketchy, and indefinite, and not very popular with our older readers. After a while he packed up and went to Australia, where I understand he became an art director in a leading Australian advertising agency. Even more sketchy and unpopular were several sets of drawings by Kurt, which my publisher had bought and foisted onto me. It never happened again.

INTERPLANETARY POLICE PATROL

Earth H.Q.:
    164 Gower St., London, N.W.1
This is to certify that

Name ....

Address ....

    ....

    ....

is a member of the
    Interplanetary Police Patrol
with the rank of

    ....

    ....

    ....

    ....

Paste your
Photograph
here

The holder of this card is entitled to
enjoy the full privileges of the I. P. P.

CAPTAIN VALIANT
C. S. I. P. P.

"FORWARD TO THE FUTURE"

Other artists who drew one or two sets of Marvelman were Dennis Gifford and Maurice Saporito. Gifford, a brilliant comic artist, was out of his element with Marvelman, whom he drew as a stylized, spindly, wooden-faced puppet, and the kids were quick in pointing this out.

There were several artists who drew Young Marvelman regularly. One, George Parlett, an ex-squadron leader and a Fleetway artist, had a lively sense of humour, a diehard British Empire attitude, and an intolerance of anybody not pukka English. Parlett's drawings had economy of line, but showed infinite and interesting detail and amazing authenticity with just a few touches. Like most of us George found it extremely difficult to meet a deadline and would turn up a page short, or say, "Can I borrow a pen for a minute. I've just got to finish off the last few frames."

Leo Rawlings, an ex-artilleryman who had been a prisoner of war of the Japanese, was a quick and fluid black and white artist whose Young Marvelman was more often than not battling the Japanese. Leo was always reliable and the kids liked his drawings. In his hands Young Marvelman never altered in appearance or lost his character and style.

Charles Baker was another Young Marvelman artist with a conscientious and practical approach to his work. His characters were always competently drawn, and his characterization of Young Marvelman never varied in style from his original interpretation. Charles was a bespectacled bachelor, middle-aged and mild-mannered, who lived on his own. After a while he left London to live near his

119

family in Norwich and came to town to see me every week. I was shocked and saddened when I heard he had taken his own life.

Stanley White, an artist of the pre-war school who had drawn strips for *Mickey Mouse Weekly*, was an ageless, perky character who always carried a pair of swimming trunks in his pocket in case he "got a chance to have a swim". His Young Marvelman was presentable enough, but everything else about his drawings had an air of quaintness that seemed to date his drawings by two or three decades. The interiors of his spaceships were equipped with early wireless sets complete with loudspeaker horns, and furnished with Victorian furniture. His characters, wide-eyed and innocent like cartoon animals, wore boots with shiny bulbous toecaps which would have done credit to any serviceman.

Whitlock sometimes drew Young Marvelman as well as Marvelman. His style, typically American, was bold, stylized, and dramatic. Don Lawrence and Roy Parker also drew Young Marvelman as well as Kid Marvelman, our replacement for Mary Marvel, in the *Marvelman Family* comic.

Other features of our Marvelman comics were adventure and Western strips, quizzes, and filler comic pages. Roy Castle, accurate in general but stiff in his figure work, had a wonderful and unusual story sense. His stories, with their accurate drawings of planes, tanks, and ships, brought in many approving letters, though his occasional Young Marvelman strips were less successful.

Stocky Peter Ford, a Maori, used to draw adventure strips in which aeroplanes often featured, and I used to take a number of Western and detective strips drawn by Spanish artists. Three of these artists – Cueto, Ramonez, and Maccabi – often had their work featured in one or more of the Marvelman titles.

Filler pages made up of one, two, or three pages of humorous strips, with as many as five pages to a comic book, were used for the Marvelman comics and some of our other titles, and the main provider of these fun pages was Dennis Gifford. He continued "The Friendly Soul" and the "Flip and Flop" series which I had started, as well as "Young Joey", in the Marvelman comics. My brother Sidney, who was at London University at the time, used to pop into the studio, which we had transferred to more salubrious premises in Hampstead Road, to draw a page of "Flip and Flop" whenever he needed a bob or two.

As well as the fillers he drew for Marvelman, Gifford also drew the fillers for most of our Western comics. We were producing complete monthly issues of *Annie Oakley*, *Davy Crockett*, *Wyatt Earp*, *Jim Bowie*, *Daniel Boone*, and *TV Heroes*, and for them Gifford drew Granny Croakley, Wynott Burp, Daniel Goone, Jim Pooey, Wild Bill Hiccup, and many others. The originals are much sought after by collectors today.

In Hampstead Road, Dorothy Saporito, a quick and competent artist, was my assistant. She inked in many covers and made coloured

Can-Can – a pin-up book of the mid-fifties.

overlays for them as well as retouching drawings and photographs. She specialized in colour work, which was brilliant. Later on, another assistant, Roshan Kanga, a capable black and white and lettering artist, drew all our titling and many half-page quizzes we featured in the Marvelman comics.

The middle and late fifties brought in more magazine work as well as comics. There were covers and editorial work on eight paperbacks (Banner Books) per month; and two Western pulp magazines; a complete package for *Flix*, a film magazine; a pocket magazine called *Can-Can*; and several detective and romance magazines. I also wrote articles for the American magazine *Mechanix Illustrated* as well as editing the English edition. In addition we produced, each year, eight annuals, four albums, and eight children's books called *Teddy Tar*.

Gower Street had been a madhouse, but compared to Hampstead Road it was a haven of rest. A photographer friend had taken the premises and kept the shop for photographic supplies and the first floor as a studio for amateur photographers, supplying equipment and models on hire. The next floor was shared by Douglas Endersby and scriptwriters Bernard Botting and Charlie Hart, who wrote "The Charlie Chester Show", and Bill Kelly, who was working on "Candid Camera". I had the top floor.

Everybody in the building wandered in and out of each other's offices, and visitors did likewise. As a conventional business house the place was a shambles, but it was a powerhouse. There were always radio and TV personalities, artists, writers, and photographic models floating around. There were little parties during the day. Everyone smoked American cigarettes at one pound a carton of two hundred and drank whisky at one pound a bottle, and if cigars were the poison preferred, King Edwards came at two pounds for a box of fifty. We lunched at Kwei's Chinese restaurant in Tottenham Court Road, at the Casa Prada, or the Delicatessen at the top of Euston Road near Great Portland Street underground station. We used to hunt for old books and magazines in Seaton Street market and buy each other birthday presents at Phillips, the stylish gents' outfitters, then in Euston Road.

When Euston Road was being widened we were all turfed out of Hampstead Road. The building was scheduled for immediate demolition. That was about fourteen years ago. The building is still standing – locked, derelict, and useless.